Leadership
TRAINING

W9-AHT-274

Includes CD-ROM with Ready-to-Use Microsoft PowerPoint® Presentations

Exercises, Handouts, Assessments, and Tools to Help You:

✔ Develop Strong Leaders at All Organizational Levels

✔ Encourage Growth of Key Leadership Competencies

✔ Become a More Effective and Efficient Facilitator

✔ Ensure Training Is on Target and Gets Results

ASTD
*Linking People,
Learning & Performance*

Lou Russell

ASTD Press is an internationally renowned source of insightful and practical information on workplace learning and performance topics, including training basics, evaluation and return-on-investment (ROI), instructional systems development (ISD), e-learning, leadership, and career development.

Ordering Information: Books published by ASTD Press can be purchased by visiting our Website at store.astd.org or by calling 800.628.2783 or 703.683.8100.

Library of Congress Catalog Card Number: 2003102325

ISBN: 1-56286-323-1

Acquisitions and Development Editor: Mark Morrow

Copyeditor: Rick Ludwick, UpperCase Publication Services, Ltd.

Interior Design and Production: Christine Cotting, UpperCase Publication Services, Ltd.

Cover Design: Charlene Osman

Cover Illustration: Todd Davidson

Printed by Victor Graphics, Inc. Baltimore, MD.
www.victorgraphics.com

The ASTD Trainer's WorkShop Series is designed to be a practical, hands-on road map to help you quickly develop training in key business areas. Each book in the series offers all the exercises, handouts, assessments, structured experiences, and ready-to-use presentations needed to develop effective training sessions. In addition to easy-to-use icons, each book in the series includes a companion CD-ROM with PowerPoint presentations and electronic copies of all supporting material featured in the book.

Other books in the Trainer's WorkShop Series:

- **New Supervisor Training**
  John E. Jones and Chris W. Chen
- **Customer Service Training**
  Maxine Kamin
- **New Employee Orientation Training**
  Karen Lawson
- **Leading Change Training**
  Jeffrey Russell and Linda Russell
- **Coaching Training**
  Chris W. Chen
- **Project Management Training**
  Bill Shackelford

Contents

There are lots of managers in the world, focusing on tasks to help businesses and governments meet their goals. There are far fewer leaders, focusing on aligning the right people to the right tasks at the right time. I do not believe that people are born into leadership. I have seen many unlikely leaders rise to the occasion when the situation merits. I believe that individually we all decide if and when it is time to commit ourselves to serving the people we will lead, and that opens us to developing the competencies required to be effective leaders. No one of us can have all the competencies at one time, but a great leader will surround himself or herself with the people who fill in the gaps. As I sit here writing in the spring of 2003, there seems to be no greater need than the need for servant leadership, a term created by Robert Greenleaf in a book with the same title. From leadership can spring collaboration, trust, and peace, sadly absent as I write.

As you use this book to teach leadership, remember that you cannot *teach* leadership. You must facilitate this class knowing full well that you are not a subject matter expert on leadership because no one is. Leadership is a journey, not a destination. Think of yourself as the chef, preparing a buffet of skills, knowledge, and challenges of leadership. The learners in your sessions, who are all at different places in their leadership journey, will decide which to take and in what portion. Your job is to keep the buffet well stocked and meet their needs. In this workshop you are a servant leader to the learners. As Greenleaf says, "Do the people being led grow?"

I have been the "queen" of Russell Martin & Associates (www.russellmartin. com) for 15 years. I currently lead Vija Dixon, Margie Brown, Carol Mason, and a dozen consultants. If you looked closely you'd see they also lead me. They are the reason I am able to write, to speak, and to facilitate learning, and

I am indebted to them. Jeff Feldman, my co-author of *IT Leadership Alchemy* that supports this workshop, and Susan Feldman, an RMA consultant who worked with Jeff and an advisory panel to develop the 10 leadership competencies in this workshop and the book, lead others daily in their pursuit of leadership. You and I are very fortunate to have their brains in our materials. Finally, great thanks to the master Thiagi whose exercises in these workshops bring leadership to life.

Thanks to my husband Doug and my daughters Kelly, Kristin, and Katherine for their patience as I constantly juggle too many things at one time. Don't we all? My husband is leader of a software company, and my daughters are leaders in different ways. Special thanks to my parents Earl and Peg Russell. My father had his own business and taught me a great deal about leading in a business setting. He is also a constant thinker, and leads others in that as well. My mother, a teacher and homemaker, taught me how to lead all the things that people don't usually notice. Whether at home, at church, or at school, she led patiently, quietly (mostly), and with great strength. The world is lucky to have an army of silent leaders who will never be on the front of the *Wall Street Journal* but who provide the engine that runs our world.

Finally, thanks to Mark Morrow and Rick Ludwick—two of the best editors and fun friends. ASTD rocks.

"One small voice can teach the world a song." – Elmo

Lou Russell
Indianapolis, Indiana
April 2003

Introduction: How to Use This Book Effectively

What's in This Chapter?

- A discussion of the value of an effective training and development program on leadership

- A process for choosing the best program for the right audience, context, and learning goals

- An explanation of how to use this workbook most effectively

- A description of what's included in this workbook and on the CD

In the last five years, business has moved through unfathomable highs, through unfathomable lows, and now seems to bounce around, not sure what will happen next. When things are going well, leadership is critical to ensure that the business is able to grab market share. In good times it is easy to get lazy and waste resources. When things are going badly, leadership is critical to ensure that the business stays viable. In bad times smaller staff and even lower budgets require careful attention. As the economy fluctuates, business strategy must fluctuate as well. None of this can occur without strong leadership at the top, but it is also required in the middle of the organization.

The Value of an Effective Training and Development Program on Leadership

You will see massive quantities of leadership books in any bookstore. If you search on the Web for leadership training, you will find hundreds of options. Virtually anyone can call himself or herself a leadership training company. Some back up their materials with research; some differentiate themselves by certification programs. Some have fancy-sounding names like "Institute" or "Academy." How can you position your work in this wide spectrum ranging from brilliant to useless?

The material in this book is based on research my company, Russell Martin & Associates, has done on leadership. In the first part of 2001, we canvassed our newsletter readers, asking them to prioritize the competencies of a good leader. Using the results of this informal survey, we set up a national advisory panel, made up of executives, middle managers, and project managers. Working with this group for more than six months, the original list was refined to the 10 that you find in this workbook. The 10 competencies are discussed in great detail in my book *IT Leadership Alchemy*. That book focuses primarily on leading technical people, but this workbook focuses on leadership for everyone. Here are the 10 Leadership Competencies:

- ◆ Self-Awareness

- ◆ Resiliency

- ◆ Working with Others: Interpersonal and Relationship Skills

- ◆ Working with Others: Communication Skills

- ◆ Working with Others: Employee Development (Coach and Motivate)

- ◆ Working with Others: Customer Orientation

- ◆ Working with Others: Strategic Business Acumen

- ◆ Working with Others: Project Leadership

- ◆ Working with Others: Creating and Actualizing Vision

- ◆ The Challenge of Change: Create, Support, and Manage Change

The audience for this book could be executive leaders, middle managers, or project managers. Another audience could be high-potential staff members who need to be developed into the next leaders as part of a succession plan. Here are some of the business problems addressed by the programs in this book:

- ◆ How can we develop our staff more effectively through their own leaders?

- ◆ How can we increase sales through better strategy implemented by the middle managers?

- ◆ How can our projects be more successful?

- ◆ How can we radically change the culture of our company?

- ◆ How can we grow our company to the next level?

◆ How can we differentiate our consulting staff when compared with so many others?

◆ How can we help our staff feel as if they are part of this company?

◆ How can we avoid downsizing? Outsourcing? Bankruptcy?

◆ How can we lead in a way that leverages diversity?

Before you begin, talk with your customers about the business problems they are trying to solve. Consider asking them which of the 10 competencies are most critical to the business situation. If you use a 360-degree assessment (see chapter 3), talking with some or all of the target learners before designing it, you will have the data to drive your choices. Leadership only makes sense in a business context—it is not effective to teach leadership as something independent of the business reality.

The programs in this workbook are designed to be experiential. No one can teach another person leadership. Leadership is something you must teach yourself. Workshops can grow skills, knowledge, and attitude. Although there are skills and knowledge components to this material, it is primarily designed to affect the attitude of the participants. In each program, the overall goal is that an individual learner will continue to choose to be a leader, growing capacity throughout his or her time in that role. There is very little lecture in this approach. Instead, you will be facilitating discussion and reflection. Don't be afraid to add your own stories and experiences because this is what will make the discussion real for your learners. It will also create an atmosphere of safety and trust, critical to this type of reflective work.

A Process for Choosing the Best Program

This book offers a number of different variations of programs from which you can choose, depending on the audience, business context, and learning goals of your customer. Table 1–1 shows these choices. The one-hour version of the program can be conducted with or without personal assessments, which increase the length by 30 minutes. The half-day version (see chapter 6) can be taught as is or you may choose to teach each of the competencies in the two-day version as individual half-day workshops. The one-day version (see chapter 7) can be taught using the material (three competencies) presented in this book or you can substitute the three competencies best suited to your customer, using the modules of the two-day version (chapter 8).

Table 1–1

An Aid to Choosing the Right Workshop Agenda

LENGTH OF MODULE	PURPOSE	LEARNING GOAL	AUDIENCE SIZE
1 hour	◆ Expose people to the concept of leadership and the 10 competencies	◆ Awareness of what leadership means ◆ Awareness of the 10 competencies	50+ people
1.5 hours	◆ Expose people to the concept of leadership and the 10 competencies ◆ Have people assess themselves to begin quantifying their own leadership journeys	◆ Awareness of what leadership means ◆ Awareness of the 10 competencies ◆ Awareness of their own strengths and gaps based on their own perceptions	50+ people
Half-day as is	◆ Expose people to the concept of leadership and the 10 competencies ◆ Have people assess themselves to begin quantifying their own leadership journeys ◆ Provide insight into their Self-Alignment (Self-Awareness and Resiliency)	◆ Awareness of what leadership means ◆ Awareness of the 10 competencies ◆ Awareness of their own strengths and gaps based on their own perceptions and behavioral assessment	30–50 people
Half-day customized	◆ Focus on one specific competency to gain skills, knowledge, and attitude change	◆ Awareness of their own gaps on this specific competency ◆ Create a development plan for the future	15–20 people
1 day as is	◆ Expose people to the concept of leadership and the 10 competencies ◆ Have people assess themselves to begin quantifying their own leadership journeys ◆ Provide insight into their own Self-Alignment (Self-Awareness and Resiliency), Communication, and Developing Others	◆ Awareness of their own strengths and gaps in these three competencies ◆ Create a development plan for the future	15–20 people

continued

Table 1–1, continued

An Aid to Choosing the Right Workshop Agenda

LENGTH OF MODULE	PURPOSE	LEARNING GOAL	AUDIENCE SIZE
1 day customized	◆ Expose people to the concept of leadership and the 10 competencies ◆ Have people assess themselves to begin quantifying their own leadership journeys ◆ Provide insight into their own Self-Alignment (Self-Awareness and Resiliency), and two other competencies based on the data from the 360-Degree Assessments	◆ Awareness of their own strengths and gaps on these specific competencies ◆ Create a development plan for the future	15–20 people
2 day as is	◆ Expose people to the concept of leadership and the 10 competencies ◆ Have people assess themselves to begin quantifying their own leadership journeys ◆ Provide insight into their own strengths and weaknesses in all 10 competencies	◆ Awareness of their own strengths and gaps for all competencies ◆ Create a development plan for the future	15–20 people

Here are the topics of the workshops as they are presented in this workbook. You can use these as you work with your customer to choose the format.

Version	Return-on-Investment
1–1.5 hours	Awareness of 10 leadership competencies, definition of leadership.
Half-day	Awareness of three categories of leadership competencies, 10 leadership competencies, definition of leadership.
One day	Awareness of individual's strengths or gaps that require improvement in four key competencies based on assessment.
Two days	Awareness of individual's strengths or gaps in all 10 competencies based on assessment; construction of a Personal Action Plan.

Whenever possible, customize the workshop to the specific needs of the audience. This is best done with assessments (see chapter 3). For the one-day version in this workbook, I have included the most common competencies from the gaps I've seen during my work, but it would be even better for you to choose the competencies based on the customer's situation.

How to Use This Workbook Most Effectively

Whether you are an experienced trainer or a novice instructor, you will find this workbook a useful resource for developing and facilitating leadership workshops. By understanding the basic concepts about the leadership competencies and then reviewing the sample training program designs, you will be able to customize the program design for a given audience.

Here's a suggestion for how to begin using this book:

- **Skim the book.** Take a quick read through the entire contents of this workbook. Study the "What's in This Chapter?" lists. Get a good sense of the layout and structure of what's included.

- **Understand the mechanics and dynamics of leadership.** Do a little research on the concept of leadership using the bibliography as a guide. Chapters 5 through 8 provide you with the background information you need to teach each of the different configurations of the program.

- **Think about the specific customer need you are trying to meet.** It is critical to have a sponsor who sees this learning as crucial to the business. Do not attempt to initiate a leadership program without a sponsor. Use table 1–1 to begin to define the amount of time and amount of customization required for your unique situation.

- **Review the methods for good training design and for creating a positive learning environment.** As you read chapter 2 you will review approaches and strategies for effectively teaching adults, preparing them for learning, supporting the "transfer" of learning to practice, and designing effective training programs. Even if you are an experienced trainer, you should find that a review of this chapter is likely to reinforce what you are probably already doing—and perhaps add to your toolkit of effective instructional design.

- **Explore the training modules.** Chapters 5 through 8 offer a variety of training programs that you can draw upon as you design a program to fit your audience.

- **Design your training program.** With your target audience defined and an awareness of the learning modules contained in this workbook, you can design your own training program.

What's in This Workbook and on the CD?

All of the assessments, training instruments, handouts, tools, and PowerPoint slides referenced in this workbook are included on the accompanying CD. Follow the instructions in the appendix, "Using the Compact Disc," at the back of the workbook or *How to Use This CD.txt* on the CD.

The training materials in this CD or book include

- tools and strategies for assessing leadership (explained in chapter 3)

- tools and strategies for evaluating the learning (explained in chapter 4)

- training workshop agendas that can be used as is or modified in response to your organization, its challenges, and your own teaching style (chapters 5–8)

- handouts, assessments, and training instruments for the learning activities that are designed to fit into the training modules (description of how to use these is in each appropriate chapter)

- Microsoft PowerPoint slides for your use in focusing the energy of workshop participants.

Please note that a number of handouts need to be used in the sample agendas. However, black-and-white versions of all the slides from the two-day workshop are on the CD. You can use any or all of these as handouts if you wish. For example, you could create a notebook for participants that contained all of these slides so they would have a reference to take away after the workshop.

Icons

For easy reference, icons are included in the margins throughout this workbook to help you quickly locate key elements in training design and instruction. Here are the icons and what they represent:

 Assessment: Appears when an agenda or learning activity includes an assessment and it identifies each assessment presented.

 CD: Indicates materials included on the CD accompanying this workbook.

 Clock: Indicates recommended timeframes for specific activities.

 Handout: Indicates handouts that you can print or copy and use to support training activities.

 **Key Point:** Alerts you to key points that you should emphasize as part of a training activity.

 Learning Activity: Identifies learning activities included in chapter 10.

 PowerPoint Item: Indicates PowerPoint presentations and slides that can be used individually. These presentations and slides are on the CD included with this workbook, and copies of the slides are included in chapters 5 through 8. Instructions for using PowerPoint slides and the CD are in appendix A.

 Tool: Identifies an item that offers useful information for facilitators.

 Training Instrument: Identifies specific materials that are used before, during, and following the training workshop.

 **What to Do Next:** Highlights recommended actions that you can take to make the transition from one section of this workbook to the next or from a specific training activity to another within a training module.

What to Do Next

- ◆ Review the next chapter to better understand your role in facilitating leadership for your organization.

- ◆ Using chapter 3, assess your own leadership competencies. Use chapter 4 to learn in more depth about each competency and develop a personal action plan for growth and leverage.

- ◆ Begin a discussion with your sponsor to define the business problem this leadership initiative will serve.

◆◆◆

The next chapter identifies the basics required to facilitate learning effectively. This includes an overview of how people learn, as well as an introduction to project management, which will be useful once you begin customizing your training solutions. In addition, it is critical for this type of learning event that you carefully reflect on the role you will play in the learning, which also is covered in chapter 2. You are not going to be the expert in leadership, pouring leadership into those who need it. You are not going to create little leader clones, all exactly alike. Instead, you will teach people to leverage their own innate strengths while shoring up some of their weaknesses. You must play the role of a leader of learning, presenting people with choices, skills, and knowledge that will allow them to choose to increase their own learning.

How People Learn

What's in This Chapter?

- ◆ How to accelerate learning for the participants

- ◆ How to customize learning development

- ◆ How trainers manage projects

- ◆ How to create a learning environment

- ◆ How to manage your role as facilitator

This chapter focuses on an individual's ability to learn more with less effort. Increased learning capacity lowers stress, reduces conflicts, and builds self-esteem. In contrast, ineffective learning increases stress, triggers blame, and challenges feelings of self-worth.

This chapter will help you review, or learn for the first time, the latest research on how people learn. As you deliver this leadership training, you will be able to adapt the materials on the spot to meet the specific needs at that time and place. This may involve throwing in some new learning activities or leaving some out, but these choices can only be made with a complete understanding of why they were there in the first place. The design of these materials is based on the research presented in this chapter. For more detailed information on these topics, refer to my book *The Accelerated Learning Fieldbook* (1999).

Accelerating Learning

In each section, there will be an opportunity for you to think about your own learning preferences. Your unique profile will consist of

- ◆ intake styles

- ◆ multiple intelligences.

Figure 2–1

Percentage of People Learning in Different Ways

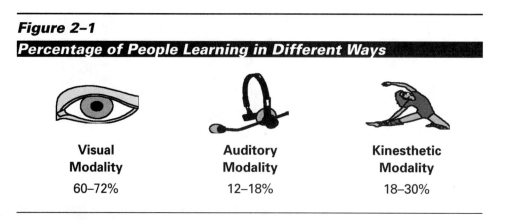

Visual Modality	Auditory Modality	Kinesthetic Modality
60–72%	12–18%	18–30%

INTAKE STYLES

Studies on how individuals prefer to get new information have been conducted for years in the field of Neuro-Linguistic Programming (NLP). These ways of learning fall into three categories, as shown in Figure 2–1.

Each learner uses a combination of these three intake styles. Some might fall strongly into one category, some have no preference between two, and some are equally able with all three. Intake styles are not the same as intelligence. Whether you prefer to learn by seeing, hearing, or doing has no bearing on how intelligent you are. It just determines your preference for receiving new learning.

It is easy to identify your own preference(s) and guess someone else's preference(s) from certain physical characteristics that track with these preferences. Visual learners prefer books or videos, tend to speak quickly and in somewhat high pitches, look up when they are thinking, and use language like, "I see what you mean." Sixty to 72 percent of the population prefers to learn this way. Auditory learners prefer speeches, discussions, or tapes; speak slowly and quietly; look straight ahead when they are thinking; and use language like, "I can hear what you are saying." They make up 12 to 18 percent of the population. Finally, kinesthetic learners prefer to try something, speak quickly with great changes in intonation and body language, look down when thinking, and use language like "I get it." Although across the general population 18 to 30 percent prefer to learn kinesthetically, I have found that there is a higher percentage of both kinesthetic and auditory preferences in technical occupations than these averages suggest. Also, training people (like you) tend to be kinesthetic.

If you are trying to communicate something new to someone (as a leader would do often), you tend to communicate in the way you personally prefer.

For example, if you are a visual learner, you will create beautiful graphics and fancy documents to communicate. But a client who is an auditory learner doesn't want the picture; he or she wants words—short and brief. This mismatch creates a barrier to communication that can often grow into conflict.

The materials and exercises for this class have been designed to speak to all three intake styles as much as possible. Get in the habit of adopting all three in your delivery style as well. For example, if you ask learners to turn to page three:

- Say, "Please turn to page three."

- Write page three in large letters on an overhead or flipchart.

- Actually turn to page three yourself.

Almost universally, information that you have only told the learners will be forgotten. Information that has been reinforced visually and kinesthetically, along with the auditory telling, will be retained more effectively.

Assessment 11–3: The Language System Diagnostic Instrument (chapter 11, page 174) is an assessment that will help you establish your own intake style preference. Your learners will also take this assessment to help them communicate more effectively in the one-day version of "Everyday Leadership."

MULTIPLE INTELLIGENCES

The intake styles reflect how people prefer to *receive* information. The multiple intelligences reflect how people prefer to *process* information (see table 2–1).

Howard Gardner, from Harvard University, has been challenging the basic beliefs about intelligence since the early 1980s. Gardner initially described a list of seven intelligences. In 1987, he added three additional intelligences to his list, and he expects the list to continue to grow. The intelligences are

- **interpersonal:** aptitude for working with others

- **logical/mathematical:** aptitude for math, logic, deduction

- **spatial/visual:** aptitude for picturing, seeing

- **musical:** aptitude for musical expression

- **linguistic/verbal:** aptitude for the written and spoken word

- **intrapersonal:** aptitude for working alone

- **bodily kinesthetic:** aptitude for being physical.

Table 2–1
The Multiple Intelligences

Choose the three or four aptitudes in which you feel you are strongest. Also select the ones you presently use most often at work and in your personal life:

Interpersonal	Intrapersonal
Logical/mathematical	Bodily/kinesthetic
Spatial/visual	Emotional
Musical	Naturalist
Linguistic/verbal	Existential

The newer intelligences are

◆ **emotional:** aptitude for identifying emotion (the basis for Daniel Goleman's books *EQ: Emotional Intelligence* and *Primal Leadership)*

◆ **naturalist:** aptitude for being with nature

◆ **existential:** aptitude for understanding one's purpose.

How does this affect your learning? Gardner believes that most people are comfortable in three or four of these intelligences and avoid the others. For example, if you are not comfortable working with others, doing group case studies may interfere with your ability to process new material. Video-based instruction will not be good for people with lower spatial/visual aptitudes. People with strong bodily/kinesthetic aptitudes need to move around while they are learning.

Allowing your learners to use their own strengths and weaknesses helps them process and learn. Here's an example: Suppose you are debriefing one of the exercises in the leadership material. The exercise has been highly interpersonal (team activity), linguistic (lots of talking), spatial/visual (the participants built an object), musical (music was playing), logical/mathematical (there were rules and structure), and kinesthetic (people moved around). You've honored all the processing styles except intrapersonal, so the people who process information in this manner probably need a return to their strength of working alone. Start the debriefing by asking people to quietly work on their own, writing down five observations of the activity. Then ask them to share as a group.

Keep an eye on the multiple intelligences throughout the learning experience. If you're starting to feel the energy dragging, it usually means that people are getting tired from trying to learn in a manner that is not best for them. Think about which intelligences have been neglected and get back to them.

Just realizing that people take in and process information differently and need different environments to maximize their learning can make a dramatic improvement in your ability to leverage participants' abilities to learn thoroughly and quickly. Attention to learning techniques can turn classroom experiences into fun spots—and speed learning in the process.

A Model for Learning Development

As you begin to teach this leadership material, you may discover that you need to develop some additional materials for an additional learning objective. To do this, it is important that you follow a process that makes sure that you honor the way people learn.

THE LEARNER FIRST APPROACH

The process this chapter will explore is called the Learner First Approach (Russell, 1999 and 2001). Figure 2–2 shows a model of this method. Because memory is strengthened by review, the mnemonic "Accelerated Learning Offers Everyone Something Magically Exciting" has been added to help you remember the seven steps. Here is a brief description of each of them.

1. **Identify the audience.** The first step is to clearly define the audience that will be affected by the learning. This will help you determine how to adapt the course to the needs of your specific learners.

2. **Identify the learning need.** In this step, the course developer needs to determine the business problem the company is trying to solve (refer to figure 2–2). Business reasons must drive learning objectives and will help you prioritize the learning objectives for each session. Not only does this approach make the learning event easier to sell; it also ensures that the money being invested in the learning event is a good return-on-investment for the company. Clarity about the business problem also guarantees that the learners will understand what is need-to-know, not just nice-to-know.

3. **Create learning objectives.** Although learning objectives are included for each variation of the leadership material in this book, you may run into a situation in which you need additional learning objectives, which will require developing supplementary materials.

Figure 2–2

The Learner First Approach

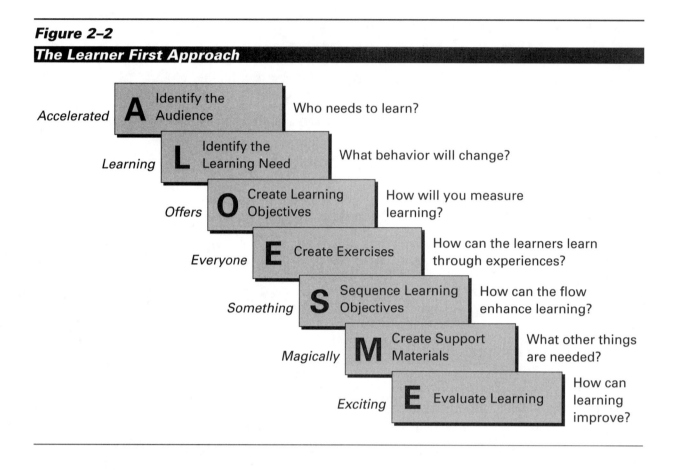

Once the business reason is clear and the needs are understood, the learning objectives can be created by clearly stating the audience and the behavior you will be able to observe during the learning event. The objectives provide guidance during the event for course developer, facilitator, and learner.

4. **Create exercises.** Whether it's running an effective meeting or climbing a mountain, people learn best when they try it themselves. The learning activities in this book allow participants to learn by doing. You may find situations in which you need to add exercises to reinforce new learning objectives.

5. **Sequence the learning objectives.** The fifth step of this approach is to determine in what order to cover the learning objectives and sequence the learning activities. A sense or intuition about sequencing comes from experience in the medium within which you are working. The sequencing for the leadership material in this book has already been done for you.

6. **Create support materials.** The next to last step of the Learner First Approach is to determine the materials you will need to supplement the exercise so that the learning objectives are achieved. Most of these have been provided for you. If you need to add material, use this list as a reminder.

    ◆ Create user, reference, and learner guides, and prerequisite work.

    ◆ Design and create the presentation media (overheads, PowerPoint slides, and so forth).

    ◆ Create the facilitator notes.

    ◆ Detail the learning event supply list.

    ◆ Design and distribute marketing information.

    ◆ Document the learning environment requirements.

7. **Evaluate the learning.** The final step is to continually monitor and make changes based on the successes, or weaknesses, of the learning event over its lifetime. Assessment ideas can be found in chapter 11 (Tool 11–3: Mini-Evaluation [page 206] to be used during class, and Tool 11–4: General Workshop Appraisal [page 207] to be used at the end of class).

Project Management for Trainers

Good project management will make the difference between success and failure as you prepare to implement your leadership learning events. There are many details that need to be considered whenever a group of learners is assembled, and the order and timing is complex and critical. In this section, you will learn a process that can be applied to any situation, whether you are offering a workshop that someone else will teach, hiring vendors to supply e-learning materials, or teaching an event yourself based on my book *Project Management for Trainers* (2000).

Dare to Properly Manage Resources

Using the mnemonic "Dare to Properly Manage Resources," you can easily remember the phases (corresponding to the first letters of each of the words in the phrase): define, plan, manage, and review (see figure 2–3). Here's an overview of each of these:

◆ **Define** answers the question, Why does the business need this work done?

◆ **Plan** answers the question, Who, what, and how will we do this project?

◆ **Manage** answers the question, How do we react to project glitches?

◆ **Review** answers the question, What did we learn about projects?

Creating a Learning Environment

In this section you will read how to maximize learning through environmental factors. Again, more detail on creating a learning environment can be found in *The Accelerated Learning Fieldbook* (Russell, 1999).

Research has shown many times that bland, neutral environments are so unlike the real world that learning achieved in these "sensory deprivation chambers" cannot be transferred to the job. Color can be a powerful way to engage the limbic part of the brain and create long-term retention. It can align the right and left brains. However, it can also trigger surprisingly negative emo-

---

Figure 2–3
The Dare Approach

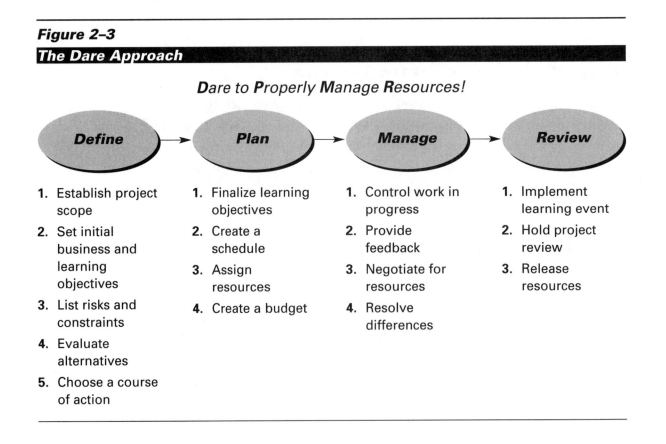

Dare to Properly Manage Resources!

Define	Plan	Manage	Review
1. Establish project scope	1. Finalize learning objectives	1. Control work in progress	1. Implement learning event
2. Set initial business and learning objectives	2. Create a schedule	2. Provide feedback	2. Hold project review
3. List risks and constraints	3. Assign resources	3. Negotiate for resources	3. Release resources
4. Evaluate alternatives	4. Create a budget	4. Resolve differences	
5. Choose a course of action			

tions, depending on each person's history, culture, and preferences. Think about the ramifications in the classroom.

Artwork, plants, and pictures that help people feel comfortable and visually stimulated are also useful. Similarly, comfortable chairs and places to write help people relax to learn. Because learning about leadership requires both individual reflection and role playing, consider seating that promotes personal thought as well as group sharing. I prefer groups of three to five at round or square tables, with each chair positioned so the projection screen can easily be seen. Leave plenty of room for each person so that when he or she does need to reflect, there is a feeling of privacy.

Having lots of flipcharts (one per table is optimal) with brightly colored markers creates an interactive environment. Consider putting colorful hard candy on the tables, with bright cups of markers, pencils, and pens. Put pads of colorful sticky notes on the table as well. I also like to bring a bag of sugar-free candy for the learners who prefer it. For the right level of trust to exist, your learners must feel as if they are honored guests.

Let music help you create an environment. Play welcoming instrumental music as people come in, preferably in a major key with a beat of about 80 beats per minute (see *The Accelerated Learning Fieldbook* for more on music use). While learners are thinking, play very quiet music at about 60 beats per minute. Play the same type of music while learners are in teams or working on exercises. Use lively music again when it is time for a break or lunch. Be careful to use music that is legal for classroom use—most is not. You will find music sources in the Resources section.

Finally, you set the environment by your attitude, the way you greet people, your clothes, and your passion. The learners will take their lead from you. You have the magic, if you use it, to help them learn.

The Roles of Learning

Before you can help someone else learn, it is critical that you understand the values that you bring to your role as learning facilitator, as depicted in figure 2–4. You will find that you play all three roles—the trainer, the facilitator, and the learner—if everything is going smoothly. In addition, you will be responsible for the logistics and process that ensure that everything comes together. To be most successful as a learning facilitator, consider the following checklist:

- Seek to clarify daily the beliefs that limit your ability to learn and, therefore, to teach.

- Learning is a gift for you, and from you, to others.

- Choose carefully what you call yourself and what you call your outcome.

- Clarify your purpose to help you better honor your roles in a learning event.

- If you can't do it with passion, don't do it.

Learning and teaching are intimately connected. If you believe learning is limited, you limit your teaching. If you believe learning is painful, you will teach with pain. If you believe that learning is liberating, your teaching will liberate others.

Figure 2-4 shows the changing roles you will juggle preparing for and delivering a learning event. When a class begins, you will play the role of trainer, bringing to the learning event a plan, structure, experience, and objectives. This will only be possible because you have a strong, repeatable logistics process. As you ask the learners to place priorities on the objectives, you will slowly release control, inviting the participants to become partners in their own learning. As you move from the trainer role into the facilitator role, the objectives are the contract between the learners and the facilitator. Little by little, control is released to the learners.

Sometimes the pendulum swings too far and the learners begin to have so much fun that they start to move away from the learning objectives. This can

Figure 2–4
The Roles of a Learning Facilitator

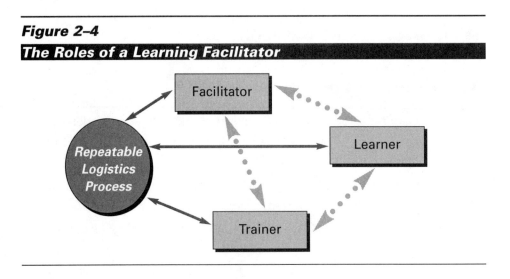

shift the workshop toward entertainment rather than education, sometimes called edu-tainment. At this point, the learning facilitator must swing the pendulum back a bit, returning to the more control-oriented role of the trainer. Control is introduced just enough to ensure alignment with the learning objectives. Throughout the entire leadership workshop, you will be balancing flexibility (facilitation) and structure (training).

There is a third role that all great facilitators play in the classroom—the role of learner. If you are open to it, you can learn many new things when you are in class. If you believe that you have to be an expert as a learning facilitator, you will not be very effective.

Summary

In this chapter, you have gained knowledge and skills to set the stage for learners to explore their own leadership strengths and weaknesses; their leadership communication with others; and their ability to align the right people, processes, and timing for the success of the company. By honoring participants' unique learning profiles; by following a clear, repeatable process to develop new material; by managing the learning event project efficiently; and, finally, by creating an optimal learning environment, you jumpstart your own ability to improve leadership learning among those you serve.

What to Do Next

- ◆ Begin your own leadership development by assessing yourself using the instructions in the next chapter.

- ◆ Using the tips and techniques in this chapter, clarify your discussion with your sponsor to define the business problem this leadership initiative will serve.

- ◆ Build a project plan for customizing this situation.

◆ ◆ ◆

With the skills and knowledge you have polished in this chapter, you are ready to build the solution that best meets the needs of your sponsor. To do this, you must first experience your own leadership strengths and challenges. The next few chapters are designed to build the depth of leadership—both for yourself and for others.

Assessing Leadership Strengths and Weaknesses

- ◆ A process for implementing a self-assessment

- ◆ A process for implementing a 360-degree assessment

- ◆ A process for implementing behavioral and motivational assessments

Leadership requires self-examination. Many people have never thought of themselves as leaders and don't really know what that means. Some think that being a good manager of tasks is leadership. It is critical to use an assessment at the beginning of your leadership sessions so that people begin to understand their own strengths and weaknesses.

It is important to emphasize here that this leadership workshop is about leveraging personal strengths, not about turning everyone into a clone of the perfect leader. There is no one person who exhibits outstanding performance in all 10 of the leadership competencies we will explore here. Leadership effectiveness depends on the leader, the people being led, and the business context. The most important leadership competencies will differ with the situation.

These assessments can be threatening but, as the facilitator, you must continue to encourage people to approach them as a way to identify strengths. Learners will tend to focus exclusively on their weaknesses, which is natural, but this can hamper leadership development. All people need to understand the areas in which they excel and then find ways to build relationships, processes, or structures that will allow them to fill in the gaps in their performance.

Certainly there are minimum levels for all the competencies. A great leader may not be the most gifted communicator, but he or she does have to be able to communicate at the level defined by the business need. The workshops are designed to provide tools for improving competencies that need growth, but also to teach people to look around them for ways to delegate the work that doesn't make the best use of their unique skills.

Three different levels of assessment are useful for this workshop. Here's the breakdown by length of workshop:

1- to 1.5-hour session	Self-assessment
Half-day session	Self-assessment
	DISC (Dominance, Influence, Steadiness, Compliance)/PIAV (Personal Interests, Attitudes, and Values) assessment (optional)
One- and two-day sessions	Self-assessment
	360-degree assessment
	DISC/PIAV assessment

As the facilitator, it is important that you complete all the assessments yourself before you teach any workshop. Each assessment is described below.

Self-Assessment

Assessment 11–1: Leadership Self-Assessment (See chapter 11, page 169) could be done at the start of class in less than 15 minutes if you have learners who have not done the advance work, which is very common. This form is also on the CD.

360-Degree Assessment

This assessment requires the most planning. If you have a 360-degree assessment tool, preferably Web-based, you will have to ask your technical staff to enter the competencies from Assessment 11–1 into the tool. Most tools prefer a numeric assessment instead of High, Medium, and Low. We use a scale of 1 to 5 for our 360-degree assessment, with 1 representing low skills (Low) and 5 representing perfect skills (High). Check the Resources section of this book for information about other Web-based 360-degree assessment options if your company does not currently have one. Assessment 11–1: Leadership Self-Assessment can also be distributed as a paper-based 360-degree assessment, but accumulating the results is more labor intensive.

In the 360-degree assessment, each participant should minimally get a number of people to assess their leadership competencies:

- ◆ Each participant needs to assess himself or herself (this will serve as the self-assessment).

- ◆ Each participant's supervisor should assess him or her. If there is a matrix reporting structure, each manager who provides input to the participant's performance review should perform an assessment.

- ◆ The participant should ask at least three peers in the organization to assess him or her.

- ◆ The participant should ask all the people who report to him or her to make an assessment. This also should include anyone whose performance review the participant influences.

The reports created by the 360-degree assessment tool will provide each participant with an average by role (supervisor, self, peers, subordinates) and in total. It will be easy to see which competencies are considered strengths and which are considered liabilities in the eyes of others. Participants will leverage the results of this assessment when they create their final action plans.

The participants will need a minimum of two weeks prior to the session to get all these people to complete the assessment. With the right Web-based tool, the assessment should take each person less than 15 minutes to complete.

Behavioral and Motivators Assessment

The purpose of assessing each individual's behavioral and motivational differences is to create a language and a model that people can use to talk about and troubleshoot differences. This self-understanding, coupled with an understanding of other peoples' styles, will help them adapt their approaches to the unique needs of the person being led.

Although we have tried many different behavioral models in our leadership practice, we prefer to use a DISC (Dominance, Influence, Steadiness, Compliance) assessment coupled with a motivator assessment called PIAV (Personal Interests, Attitudes, and Values) (see Assessment 11–2 on page 172). If you are an independent training company, contact www.tti.com to get information about becoming a distributor. If you are not an independent training company, check the Resources section of this book for nformation on acquiring these assessments. If your company has other assessments that it prefers, you will need to replace the pages and PowerPoint slides on DISC and PIAV in the chapters with the model that you are using.

Participants need a full five days before class to get these assessments done, although the DISC and PIAV assessments take a total of less than 20 minutes to complete.

Privacy Issues

Both the 360-degree assessment and DISC/PIAV assessments contain personal information that should never be shared with anyone without both the participants' permission and that of their bosses. If you intend to share the assessment with others, it is critical that you inform people that you will be doing that before they take the assessments.

Depending on the situation, you may find that you have copies of assessment results that you will need to archive so you can distribute them to your learners. Be aware that these files need to be properly secured and even printed reports that are not used should be disposed of in a highly secure way (we recommend shredding). Check with your human resources department for your company's legal and business requirements.

Summary

The first competencies required to grow leadership are those concerned with self-understanding. Change cannot occur until understanding does. The assessments discussed in this chapter are the building blocks of the learning experience. Although it does require coordination and a great deal of work, fight to get people to give these assessments the energy they require. Without them, your leadership session will be merely an academic exercise.

 ## What to Do Next

- ◆ Use chapter 4 to learn more about each competency, and develop a personal action plan for growth and leverage.

- ◆ Using your discussions with your sponsor as your guide, design the right amount of assessment for this business problem. To adequately debrief the assessments, a minimum of a day is required.

◆   Read the teaching guide and slides for the workshop that makes the most sense based on your earlier analysis.

◆ ◆ ◆

With clarification about your role in the classroom and an understanding of the uniqueness of your own leadership, you will be ready to delve into each competency in more depth to prepare yourself to customize training according to the needs of your business customer.

Evaluation

There are two components to measuring the success of a learning event—the effectiveness of the workshop itself and the benefit to the business. It is possible to hold a highly popular workshop with virtually no business benefit. On the other hand, it is less likely but still possible to hold a very unpopular workshop with good business results.

The business reason or situation that caused the request for learning is key to the measurement of effectiveness after the program has been completed. For this reason it is critical that you establish the learning objectives with your sponsor before any design begins. The workshops included in this book have learning objectives, but if you are customizing the material, you need to customize the learning objectives as well.

Once the business reason is clear and the needs are understood, the learning objectives can be created by clearly stating the audience and the behavior you will be able to observe during the learning event. The objectives provide direction for course developer, facilitator, and learner. They are the core around which the entire learning experience is built and they provide your contract with your sponsor.

Creating learning objectives can be time-consuming. To simplify the process, here is a pared-down version of more academic approaches to creating objectives. In this section, you will learn how to create good learning objectives by specifying the audience, behavior, condition, and degree.

- ◆ **Audience (A):** Who will be learning? To whom is this objective geared? (See the first step of The Learner First Approach).

- ◆ **Behavior (B):** What will the learner be able to do differently and how? How will the facilitator know?

- ◆ **Condition (C):** What will the environment be where the learning is needed? (See the second step of The Learner First Approach).

- ◆ **Degree (D):** What amount (degree) of performance is required by the business?

Here's an example of why material tailored to a specific audience matters so much. Suppose you have a need to learn project management skills. You are given the choice of attending either a five-day public workshop with 100 other learners or a one-on-one session for a day with the informal guru of project management at your company. Personality issues aside, most learners would pick the guru if they felt they had a true need to learn. Why? There is no time in business today to sort through a lot of information that is not relevant to your situation. Learners want *their* questions answered, not someone else's. Trying to create a workshop for all people, as does a generic project management class, runs the risk that the learning will be degraded for everyone.

Good facilitators really want the learners to learn. But learning can take many forms and can happen in different degrees and with different progressions. For example, not everyone at your company needs to be an expert at coaching. Your business likely requires that the supervisors be experts, but staff with no direct reports don't really need this competency. The learning event created for a specific audience must facilitate learning for staff members at the degree required by the business. Focus the learning objective on the three types of learning that can occur.

1. Will the learner have a new *skill?* Will the learner be able to do something new?

2. Will the learner have new *knowledge?* What level of expertise will the learner have?

3. Will the learner have a new *attitude?* Will the learner have a new belief?

Most learning in business requires all three, but attitude is the most prevalent need and the most difficult learning to facilitate. Let's say your business has a group of managers who are having problems managing their projects. Their bosses would like the managers to be taught how to get projects done on time, with high quality and within budget. More important, they would like the managers to choose to spend time applying new (or perhaps old) skills and knowledge to make this occur. The biggest behavioral change is the desire to improve project management. In fact, if the managers don't believe in project management, they will never open up enough to learn the knowledge and skills.

When you ask your customers to describe how behaviors will change after a learning event, many will list skills and knowledge, forgetting about attitude. As you gather the needs, ask questions to ensure that the customers have considered all of the learning needs.

The learning objectives describe the behavior change desired from the learner after the learning event. Each objective includes an action verb. It is something the *learner* will do, not something the facilitator or someone else will do. It is something that the learner can demonstrate and the facilitator can observe. It is something that is needed by the business for the learner to be more valuable. Learning objectives are concerned with observable behavior, so use good action verbs.

The condition specifies what the environment will be when the learner demonstrates the behavior. Put in more real-world terms, the condition describes what will be in the work environment as the behavior is performed, such as

- What tools will be used during the application of the newly learned behavior?

- What timing or sequencing is required?

- What job aids will be available to help?

- What equipment will be used?

- What things are not dependable?

Sometimes conditions make a lot of sense, but they aren't always needed. Putting arbitrary conditions in a learning objective is as detrimental as having no learning objective. For example, adding a condition to the end of this example doesn't help at all: After completing the workshop, the supervisor will be able to apply the five coaching questions to a job feedback session while sitting at a desk.

You may also need to specify how proficient the learners need to be in their new behavior. Often there is a requirement to be able to perform in a specific amount of time or to a specific level of quality. An example might be the following: The customer service representative will enter completely correct orders into the accounts receivable system 75 percent of the time. Put another way, 25 percent of the time an order entered into the business system will be inaccurate. The practice and reinforcement that goes on in a workshop that is shooting for 75 percent accuracy is different from the learning for a 100 percent or even a 20 percent accuracy.

There is a wonderful saying: "We value what we measure." There are many ridiculous stories of how the wrong metrics and measurements can accidentally create behavior in individuals and teams that is counterproductive to the needs of the company. Specifying a meaningless degree of measurement in a learning objective has the same effect. If the learning objectives are wrong, so is the learning.

Training managers can easily track the long-term value of training when a degree is specified. Learning objectives can be mapped to dollars in added productivity from hours saved. For example, if a customer service representative raises her productivity from 50 percent to 75 percent, there is a real return in dollars.

However, it is often very difficult to specify degree. How do you measure the accuracy of a person's time management ability or leadership ability? In some cases it may be possible to use a comparison to quantify the learning objectives that are hard to measure. For example: The supervisor will be able to list his or her top three leadership strengths when compared to a list of Abraham Lincoln's leadership characteristics.

There has been a tendency on the part of some overly ambitious course developers to embed meaningless measurements in their objectives. Often this is a marketing ploy, not a learning enabler. For example: The trainer will learn 47 ways to open a workshop. Forty-seven has no relevance to a real-world learning gap. Why not 23? 14? 3? Learners resent learning objectives that sound irrelevant, disconnected, and oriented to marketing.

Mini-Evaluation for Longer Workshops

Many trainers measure the effectiveness of the workshop at the end. This prevents them from adjusting before it is too late to fix the problems. A mini-evaluation can be used partway through a session, or even multiple times, giving the facilitator a chance to make adjustments. See Tool 11–3: Mini-Evaluation for a sample of this type of evaluation.

The mini-evaluation is only appropriate for the one-day or longer version of the training program. Ask people to complete the anonymous evaluation quickly and return it to you at a break (usually in the morning or at lunch). At the first break, summarize the results on a flipchart. This gives the learners the opportunity to see what others said, helping them understand that their opinions may not always be the same as others. Majority rules in this evaluation, and learners appreciate that.

Evaluations for Workshop Completion

We like to use an evaluation like Tool 11–4: General Workshop Appraisal at the end of a session. Notice that the two parts of the appraisal have different perspectives. The first part focuses on the delivery techniques of the facilitator, and is mostly ranking. I call this the "left brain" side. The second part focuses on other potential workshop topics and possible other attendees to the workshop just completed. I tell learners this is the "right brain" side of the evaluation.

These evaluations don't really tell you how much people have learned because, with leadership, it is certainly too soon to tell. However, they do tell you the learners' attitude toward the content and what they'll tell others about the program.

If you have the access, consider asking participants to make another evaluation or something similar 30 to 60 days after the workshop. This will give you more information about perceived long-term retention. In addition, consider contacting the supervisors of the learners 30 days or more after the session to see if they've seen behavioral change.

Evaluation of Business Benefit

Business benefit is based on the answer to a three-part question: Did the investment increase revenue, avoid cost, or improve the service of the business? Early in development, it is critical that you help your sponsor ensure that the learning objectives contribute to a business strategy designed to do one of these three things. Truly measuring business benefit will require the participation of the sponsor. Leadership growth can be started with training, but it is unlikely without change in job descriptions, incentive, processes, and relationships. All of these must be measured to ensure business benefit.

What to Do Next

- ♦ Using your discussions with your sponsor as your guide, finalize some business outcomes that can be measured after the training.

- ♦ Finalize your implementation strategy for your customers.

◆

One-Hour Program

- ◆ The teaching notes for presenting 1 to 1.5 hours of overview material on leadership

- ◆ Criteria for adjusting from 1 to 1.5 hours

You may have opportunities to do "sneak previews" of the leadership program, such as this one. However, realize that no one can improve their leadership performance after an exposure of only an hour or so. The learning objectives of this unit involve awareness. The main purpose of this short presentation is to get participants thinking about who they are as leaders in order to set goals for beginning a leadership development journey. The times noted in parentheses reflect how long that segment will take.

One-Hour Program

OBJECTIVES

The objectives of the one-hour program are to

- ◆ acknowledge that personal values and leadership styles are unique and diverse

- ◆ identify the 10 competencies of leadership

- ◆ create an individual goal for leveraging participants' individual leadership strengths.

MATERIALS

For the instructor:

- ◆ This chapter for reference

- ◆ Learning Activity 10–1: Understanding Leadership

- Learning Activity 10–5: Behavioral Style

- Learning Activity 10–23: The Big Close

- PowerPoint slides: "Everyday Leadership" (slides 1–10). To access slides for this program, open the file *One-Hour.ppt* on the accompanying CD. Copies of the slides for this training session are included on pages 39 to 40.

For the participants:

- Assessment 11–1: Leadership Self-Assessment

- Assessment 11–2: Quick n' Dirty DISC/PIAV Assessment

- Training Instrument 11–1: Action Plan

Using the CD

Materials for this training session are provided in this workbook and as electronic files on the accompanying CD. To access the electronic files, insert the CD and click on the appropriate Adobe .pdf document. Further directions and help with using the files can be found in Appendix A, "Using the Compact Disc."

One-Hour Sample Agenda

The times assigned to the elements of this training are approximate and will vary with discussion and trainer emphasis.

8:00 a.m. Welcome (5 minutes)

Welcome the participants to the program. Begin the session immediately with an interactive experience, by showing the Everyday Leadership, Session Contents, and Course Objectives PowerPoint slides (slides 5–1, 5–2, 5–3).

8:05 Learning Activity 10–1: Understanding Leadership (chapter 10, page 108) (20 minutes)

This exercise introduces leadership concepts and provides an opportunity to understand the 10 basic competencies of leadership. The participants will experience different forms of leadership, as well as different strengths and weaknesses, during this activity.

8:25   What is Leadership? (5 minutes)

Show PowerPoint slide 5–4. Explain the groupings of Self-Alignment, Working with Others, and Integration, and note the competencies contained in each. Explain that growing leadership requires that we explore ourselves, learn to work well with others, but most importantly learn to integrate the right tools and techniques, with the right people, for the right task, at the right time. This is the magic of leadership.

8:30   Introducing the Leadership Competencies (15 minutes)

Show PowerPoint slides 5–5 and 5–6, the 10 leadership Competencies.

Now distribute Assessment 11–1: Leadership Self-Assessment (chapter 11, page 169). If you are only doing a one-hour presentation, assign this as homework. If you are presenting a 1.5-hour session, ask the learners to complete this exercise in the session. Play quiet instrumental music while participants work on their own.

8:45   Learning Activity 10–5: Behavioral Style (chapter 10, page 115) (20 minutes)

The two assessments used in this activity compose a non-scientific way to determine how each learner behaves and how others would describe the behavior, as well as what appeals to each learner and what he or she avoids.

9:05   Action Plan (20 minutes)

Distribute and discuss Training Instrument 11–1: Action Plan (chapter 11, page 179). If you have time, ask learners to take a couple of minutes to respond to the questions in the instrument. If you are doing the 90–minute version of the program, there will be time for people to spend 20 minutes on this. If you are doing the one-hour version, assign this for homework.

9:25   Learning Activity 10–23: The Big Close (chapter 10, page 144)

This is a good way to end your session on an upbeat note.

What to Do Next

- ◆ Prepare for the one-hour course.

- ◆ Build a detailed plan to prepare for this session, including schedule and room reservations, invitations, supply list, teaching notes, and time estimate.

- ◆ Evaluate the effectiveness of the program using the ideas in chapter 4.

Slide 5–1

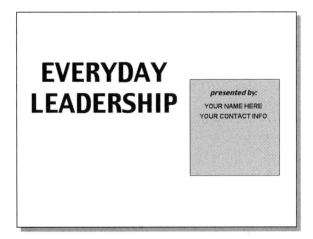

Slide 5–2

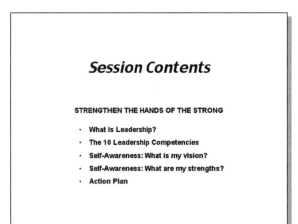

Slide 5–3

Slide 5–4

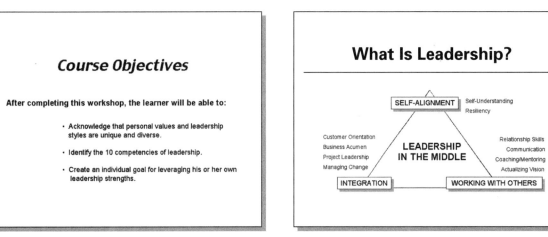

Slide 5–5

Slide 5–6

Slide 5–7

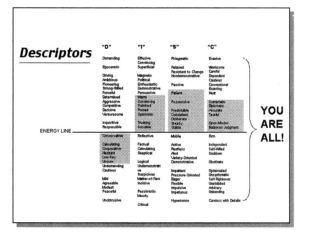

Slide 5–8

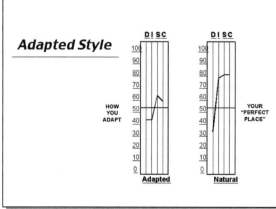

Slide 5–9

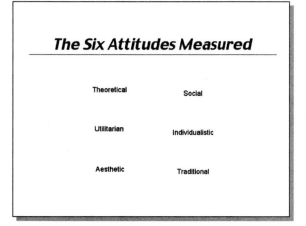

The Six Attitudes Measured

Theoretical	Social
Utilitarian	Individualistic
Aesthetic	Traditional

Slide 5–10

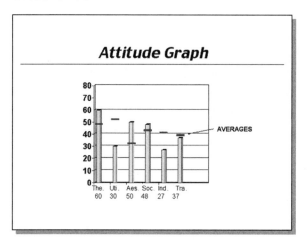

Half-Day Program

What's in This Chapter?

- Objectives for presenting a half-day of overview material on leadership
- Detailed program agenda
- Criteria for using any of the two-day workshop modules as stand-alone half-day modules

In this chapter you will learn to facilitate two different half-day versions of the leadership material. The first version, with notes for the PowerPoint presentation, focuses on introducing learners to the competencies of Self-Alignment: Self-Understanding and Resiliency. I believe that these are the first competencies that must be addressed. Jumping into the Working with Others or Integration competencies will not be as successful without first doing the inner work of Self-Alignment.

That said, you might be asked to conduct a half-day program focused on one specific competency after learners have attended the one- or two-day overview versions of the leadership workshop. There are instructions at the end of this chapter for customizing this kind of half-day learning event.

Half-Day Program

OBJECTIVES

The objectives for the half-day leadership training workshop are to

- acknowledge that personal values and leadership styles are unique and diverse
- identify the 10 competencies of leadership

◆ create an individual goal for leveraging participants' own leadership strengths.

MATERIALS

For the instructor:

◆ This chapter for reference

◆ Learning Activity 10–3: Personal Mission

◆ Learning Activity 10–4: Self-Assessment

◆ Learning Activity 10–5: Behavioral Style

◆ Learning Activity 10–6: Resiliency Attitude

◆ Learning Activity 10–23: The Big Close

◆ PowerPoint slides: "Everyday Leadership" (slides 1–9). To access slides for this program, open the file *Half-Day.ppt* on the accompanying CD. Copies of the slides for this training session are included at the end of this chapter on pages 46 and 47.

◆ Flipchart and marking pens

For the participants:

◆ Handout 11–1: The 10 Leadership Competencies

◆ Assessment 11–1: Leadership Self-Assessment

◆ Assessment 11–2: Quick n' Dirty DISC/PIAV Assessment

◆ Training Instrument 11–1: Action Plan

 Using the CD

Materials for this training session are provided in this workbook and as electronic files on the accompanying CD. To access the electronic files, insert the CD and click on the appropriate Adobe .pdf document. Further directions and help in locating and using the files can be found in Appendix A, "Using the Compact Disc."

Half-Day Sample Agenda

The times assigned to the elements of this training are approximate and will vary with discussion and trainer emphasis.

9:00 a.m.   Welcome (5 minutes)

Show PowerPoint slide 6–1 as the participants enter. When all are seated, show PowerPoint slides 6–2 and 6–3. Review the agenda and objectives. Explain that this half-day program will explore the learners' own competencies and beliefs about their leadership roles. Emphasize that the goal is to identify unique strengths so they can be leveraged in the unique leadership role of each individual rather than turning everyone into clones.

Explain that the tendency will be to focus on the weaknesses or gaps, but these will only be explored in order to grow them to a "good enough," minimal competency. In other words, the idea is to "strengthen the hands of the strong."

As facilitator, you will have to work very diligently at keeping the focus away from "how flawed I am."

9:05   Learning Activity 10–3: Personal Mission (chapter 10, page 112) (30 minutes)

In this exercise each learner will work alone to come up with three nouns and a verb to describe his or her personal mission. Help them understand that a personal mission is a statement of why they are on Earth. This works best if you go first, sharing your own personal mission statement.

Once they have had a few minutes to think, ask each person to introduce himself or herself (with job and company if appropriate) and share his or her personal mission.

9:35   Learning Activity 10–4: Self-Assessment (chapter 10, page 114) (20 minutes)

This exercise will start people thinking about their own strengths and weaknesses as leaders.

Pass out Handout 11–1: The 10 Leadership Competencies. This will provide students with a copy to use in the activities so they will not have to keep their personal self-assessments out for all to see. Explain that this half-day version of the program will focus on the competencies of Self-Understanding and Resilience.

9:55   Break (15 minutes)

10:10   Learning Activity 10–5: Behavioral Style (chapter 11, page 115) (35 minutes)

The two assessments used in this activity compose a non-scientific way to determine how each learner behaves and how others would describe the behavior, as well as what appeals to each learner and what he or she avoids.

10:45   Break (15 minutes)

11:00   Learning Activity 10–6: Resiliency Attitude (chapter 10, page 119) (20 minutes)

This is an exercise to emphasize how much attitude influences resiliency. Move into this quickly because people will be reluctant at first to participate. Notice different people's reactions so you can share them during the debriefing.

11:20   Master Strategies (5 minutes)

Show the Master Strategies slide (slide 6–9). This illustrates that this workshop has given the participants a compass to align their plan to grow leadership, so they know what really matters to them. It has also given them a map of strengths and places for improvement. Their attitude and personal choice (resilience) will help them succeed on this journey. This might be a good time to share with them resources for additional learning on any of these.

11:25   Action Plan (15 minutes)

Distribute and discuss Training Instrument 11–1: Action Plan. Explain that they will not have time to finish, but should return to this later to review and reinforce their leadership journeys. Give them a few minutes to reflect on the questions.

11:40   Learning Activity 10–23: The Big Close (chapter 10, page 144) (10 minutes)

This is a good way to end your session on an upbeat note.

The Customized Half-Day Version

Each of the units in the two-day workshop can be used as stand-alone units. In general, two competencies (two units) can be shared in a half-day session, but check the timing of teaching notes in the two-day version for actual times. Remember to adjust your discussion of the agenda and objectives to reflect the competencies you have chosen.

What to Do Next

- ◆ Build a detailed plan for preparing for this session, including schedule and room reservations, invitations, supply list, teaching notes, and time estimate.

- ◆ Plan how to implement an Action Plan for the learners, using chapter 9 as a guide.

- ◆ Implement these plans.

- ◆ Evaluate the effectiveness of the program using the ideas in chapter 4.

Slide 6–1

EVERYDAY LEADERSHIP

presented by:
YOUR NAME HERE
YOUR CONTACT INFO

Slide 6–2

Session Contents

STRENGTHEN THE HANDS OF THE STRONG

- **What is Leadership?**
- **The 10 Leadership Competencies**
- **Self-Awareness: Personal Mission**
- **Self-Awareness: What are my strengths?**
- **Resiliency**
- **Action Plan**

Slide 6–3

Course Objectives

After completing this workshop, the learner will be able to:

- Acknowledge that personal values and leadership styles are unique and diverse.
- Identify the 10 competencies of leadership.
- Create an individual goal for leveraging his or her own leadership strengths.

Slide 6–4

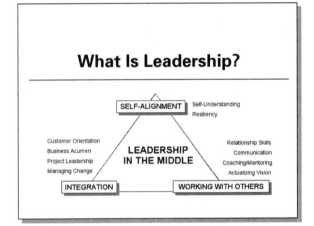

Slide 6–5

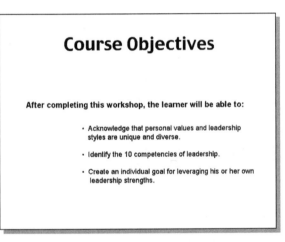

Slide 6–6

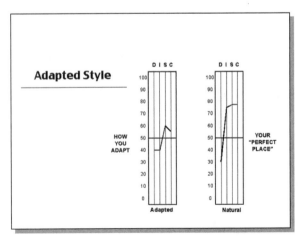

Slide 6–7

The Six Attitudes Measured

Theoretical	Social
Utilitarian	Individualistic
Aesthetic	Traditional

Slide 6–8

Attitude Graph

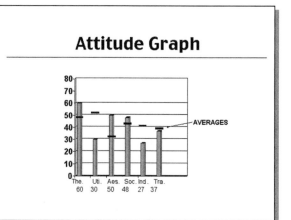

Slide 6–9

Master Strategies:
Living in a World of Permanent Whitewater

Operating in our world of rapid, tumultuous, unrelenting change has been compared to running a raging, white water river. Here are some things to remember for navigating the river of change without getting swamped ...

- Remember to pack your attitude.
- Don't look where you don't want to go.
- Go with the flow.
- Explore what's around the next bend.
- Take time to eddy out.

Life is change.
Growth is Optional.

One-Day Program

- Objectives and teaching notes for presenting a one-day workshop stressing the competencies of Self-Alignment, Communication, and Developing Others

- Detailed program agenda

- Criteria for customizing a one-day workshop stressing the competency of Self-Alignment, with two additional competencies chosen by the customer

The one-day noncustomized version of the leadership workshop is designed to expose people to the Self-Alignment competencies and then give them more depth in Coaching and Communication, two common gaps in leadership abilities. In the customized one-day version, you choose which competencies to cover in the afternoon, based on pre-class assessments.

In both the customized and noncustomized versions of the one-day workshop, the first half-day exactly duplicates the half-day noncustomized version described in the preceding chapter. The difference occurs in the afternoon. If you are able to have the learners use the list of competencies in Assessment 11–1 (chapter 11, page 169) for a 360-degree assessment, and can have the results from this a bit ahead of time, you will choose the two "lowest" competencies of the entire group for the afternoon's focus. There will be more detail on this approach at the end of this chapter. If you are not able to do 360-degree assessments in advance, use the teaching notes and the noncustomized version below. Based on our research and teaching experiences, Communication and Developing Others (feedback and coaching) are generally the competencies with which most people need some help, so those competencies are in this version.

The first half-day duplicates the material from the half-day version, which includes introducing learners to the competencies of Self-Alignment: Self-Understanding and Resiliency. I believe that these are the first competencies that must be addressed. Jumping into the Working With Others or Integration competencies will not be as successful without first doing the inner work of Self-Awareness.

One-Day Program

TRAINING OBJECTIVES

The objectives for the one-day leadership training workshop are to

- acknowledge that personal values and leadership styles are unique and diverse

- identify the 10 competencies of leadership

- create an individual goal for leveraging participants' own leadership strengths

- identify how to improve participants' own communication abilities

- begin to learn techniques for developing others.

MATERIALS

For the instructor:

- This chapter for reference

- Learning Activity 10–3: Personal Mission

- Learning Activity 10–4: Self-Assessment

- Learning Activity 10–5: Behavioral Style

- Learning Activity 10–6: Resiliency Attitude

- Learning Activity 10–7: Intake Styles

- Learning Activity 10–10: Coaching Role Play

- Learning Activity 10–14: Feedback

- Learning Activity 10–23: The Big Close

- PowerPoint slides: "Everyday Leadership" (slides 1–21 beginning on page 57). To access slides for this program, open the file *One-Day.ppt* on the accompanying CD. Copies of the slides for this training session are included at the end of this chapter.

For the participants:

- ◆ Handout 11–1: The 10 Leadership Competencies

- ◆ Handout 11–2: Chuck's Role

- ◆ Handout 11–3: Angela's Role

- ◆ Handout 11–4: Observation Checklist

- ◆ Handout 11–5: A Difficult Conversations Checklist

- ◆ Handout 11–12: Feedback

- ◆ Handout 11–13: Hints and Solutions for Feedback

- ◆ Assessment 11–1: Leadership Self-Assessment

- ◆ Assessment 11–2: Quick n' Dirty DISC/PIAV

- ◆ Assessment 11–3: The Language System Diagnostic Instrument

- ◆ Training Instrument 11–1: Action Plan

- ◆ Training Instrument 11–10: Performance Review

Using the CD

Materials for this training session are provided in this workbook and as electronic files on the accompanying CD. To access the electronic files, insert the CD and click on the appropriate Adobe .pdf document. Further directions and help in locating and using the files can be found in Appendix A, "Using the Compact Disc."

One-Day Sample Agenda

9:00 a.m.   Welcome (5 minutes)

Show PowerPoint slide 7–1 as the participants enter. When they are all seated, show slides 7–2 and 7–3. Review the agenda and objectives. Explain that this one-day program will explore the learners' own competencies and beliefs about their own leadership roles. Emphasize that the goal is to identify unique strengths so they can be leveraged in the unique leadership role of each individual rather than turning everyone into clones.

Explain that the tendency will be to focus on the weaknesses or gaps, but these will only be explored in order to grow them to a "good enough," minimal competency. In other words, the idea is to "strengthen the hands of the strong."

As facilitator, you will have to work very diligently at keeping the focus away from "how flawed I am."

9:05　Learning Activity 10–3: Personal Mission (chapter 10, page 112) (30 minutes)

In this exercise, each learner will work alone to come up with three nouns and a verb to describe his or her personal mission. Help them understand that a personal mission is a statement of why they are on Earth. This works best if you go first, sharing your own personal mission statement.

Once they have had a few minutes to think, ask each person to introduce himself or herself (with job and company if appropriate) and share his or her personal mission.

9:35　Learning Activity 10–4: Self-Assessment (chapter 10, page 114) (20 minutes)

This exercise will start people thinking about their own strengths and weaknesses as leaders.

Pass out Handout 11–1: The 10 Leadership Competencies (chapter 11, page 148). This will provide students with a copy to use in all the activities so they will not have to keep their personal self-assessments out for all to see. Explain that this part of the program will focus on the competencies of Self-Understanding and Resilience.

9:55　Break (15 minutes)

10:10　Learning Activity 10–5: Behavioral Style (chapter 10, page 115) (35 minutes)

The two assessments used in this activity compose a non-scientific way to determine how each learner behaves and how others would describe the behavior, as well as what appeals to each learner and what he or she avoids.

10:45   Break (15 minutes)

11:00   Learning Activity 10–6: Resiliency Attitude (chapter 10, page 119) (20 minutes)

This is an exercise to emphasize how much attitude influences resilience. Move into this quickly because people will be reluctant at first to participate. Notice different people's reactions so you can share them during the debriefing.

11:20   Master Strategies (5 minutes)

Show the Master Strategies slide (slide 7–9). This illustrates that this workshop will give the participants a compass to align their plan to grow leadership, so they know what really matters to them. It will also give them a map of strengths and places for improvement. Their attitude and personal choice (resilience) will help them succeed on this journey. This might be a good time to share resources for additional learning on any of these.

11:25   Action Plan (5 minutes)

Distribute and discuss Training Instrument 11–1: Action Plan (chapter 11, page 179). Explain that they will not have time to finish, but should return to this later to review and reinforce their leadership journey. Give them a few minutes to reflect on the questions.

11:30   Shared learning (25 minutes)

Toss a Koosh ball around and ask each person to share one thing they've learned about leadership. Safety rules: make eye contact, say person's name, toss underhand.

11:55   Lunch (65 minutes)

1:00 p.m.   Learning Activity 10–7: Intake Styles (chapter 10, page 121) (30 minutes)

Use slide 7–10 to debrief the learners' assessments.

1:30   Learning Activity 10–10: Coaching Role Play (chapter 10, page 126) (45 minutes)

This exercise gives the learners a chance to practice everything that has been discussed in the session.

2:15   Break (15 minutes)

2:30   Therapy Versus Coaching (5 minutes)

Use slide 7–11 to emphasize the difference between therapy and coaching: therapy goes back, coaching goes forward. Explain that the flow is to establish a gap in abilities, establish goals to close that gap, and work on implementing an action plan. Explain that the coach's role is to be a mirror—facilitating the direction that is being discovered by the person being coached.

2:40   Coaching Language (15 minutes)

Read through slide 7–12 together, and then ask the learners to silently read through slide 7–13. Ask for volunteers to restate the "not" phrases on slide 7–12 in better coaching language, using the guidelines on slide 7–13. Show PowerPoint slide 7–14 and give the participants a minute to read this.

2:55   Performance Review Coaching (10 minutes)

Show slide 7–15 and distribute Training Instrument 11–10: Performance Review (chapter 11, page 189) as a resource for use before and after a performance review coaching session to help monitor its effectiveness. Ask the learners to read through the list and put a star next to something they already do well and a circle around something they would like to do next time or improve. Ask for volunteers to share their strengths and weaknesses, but do not force all to participate.

3:05   Avoiding Conflict (5 minutes)

Quickly go over slides 7–16 and 7–17, which translate the coaching language into language that avoids provoking conflict. Emphasize the importance of "I" versus "You" language. Use examples from the Feedback learning activity to emphasize the points on this page.

3:10   Learning Activity 10–14: Feedback (chapter 10, page 132) (30 minutes)

This is a fun exercise based on a frame game developed by Thiagi to help learners begin to think about communication, leadership, coaching, and feedback. (Check the Resources section for more information on Thiagi's resources)

3:40   Difficult Feedback (10 minutes)

Slide 7–18 shares techniques for accepting difficult feedback. Sometimes in a leadership situation, people will lash back at you. It's important to control your initial emotional reaction, to "seek first to understand" by applying these stalling and calming techniques.

Ask for volunteers to demonstrate each of these techniques while you role-play someone who has approached the volunteer and said, "I knew this would happen. I never wanted to be on a project with someone like you!" Distribute Handout 11–5: A Difficult Conversations Checklist (chapter 11, page 153). Review the feedback lessons learned using slides 7–19 and 7–20.

3:50   Break (15 minutes)

4:05   Action Plan (15 minutes)

Ask the learners to return to Training Instrument 11–1: Action Plan (chapter 11, page 179) and continue filling in their thoughts from the afternoon's material. After they have done this, again toss a Koosh ball around and ask each person to share one thing they've learned about leadership.

4:20   Finish with Learning Activity 10–23: The Big Close (chapter 10, page 144). This is the same close as is used in the half-day and shorter versions.

The One-Day Customized Version

As mentioned earlier, if you are able to have the learners use the list of leadership competencies for a 360-degree assessment, and can have the results from this a bit ahead of time, you can choose the two "lowest" competencies of the entire group for the afternoon's focus. Each of the units in the two-day workshop can be used as a stand-alone unit. An option that works, although not quite as effectively, is to have each of the learners assess himself or herself against the competencies ahead of time, and use these data to pick the competencies for the afternoon. In general, two competencies (two units) can be shared in a half-day, but check the timing of the teaching notes in the two-day version for actual times. Remember to adjust the agenda and objectives to reflect the competencies you have chosen.

What to Do Next

- ◆ Using the material in chapter 2 as a guide, build a detailed plan to prepare for this session, including schedule and room reservations, invitations, supply list, teaching notes, and time estimate.

- ◆ Plan how to implement an Action Plan for the learners, using chapter 9 as a guide.

- ◆ Implement these plans.

- ◆ Evaluate the program's effectiveness using the ideas in chapter 4.

Slide 7–1

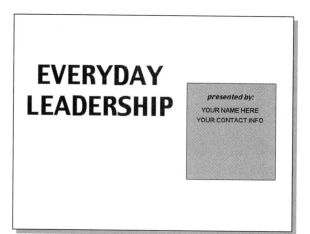

EVERYDAY LEADERSHIP

presented by:
YOUR NAME HERE
YOUR CONTACT INFO

Slide 7–2

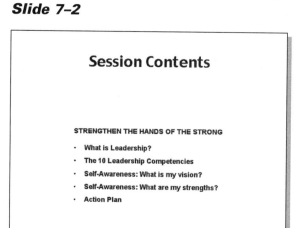

Session Contents

STRENGTHEN THE HANDS OF THE STRONG

- What is Leadership?
- The 10 Leadership Competencies
- Self-Awareness: What is my vision?
- Self-Awareness: What are my strengths?
- Action Plan

Slide 7–3

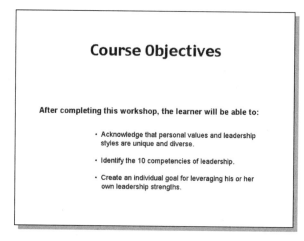

Course Objectives

After completing this workshop, the learner will be able to:

- Acknowledge that personal values and leadership styles are unique and diverse.
- Identify the 10 competencies of leadership.
- Create an individual goal for leveraging his or her own leadership strengths.

Slide 7–4

What Is Leadership?

SELF-ALIGNMENT — Self-Understanding, Resiliency

Customer Orientation
Business Acumen
Project Leadership
Managing Change

LEADERSHIP IN THE MIDDLE

Relationship Skills
Communication
Coaching/Mentoring
Actualizing Vision

INTEGRATION

WORKING WITH OTHERS

Slide 7–5

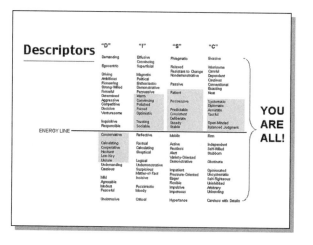

Slide 7–6

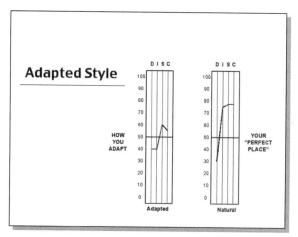

Adapted Style

Slide 7–7

The Six Attitudes Measured

Theoretical	Social
Utilitarian	Individualistic
Aesthetic	Traditional

Slide 7–8

Attitude Graph

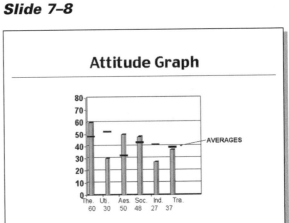

Slide 7–9

Master Strategies:
Living in a World of Permanent Whitewater

Operating in our world of rapid, tumultuous, unrelenting change has been compared to running a raging, white water river. Here are some things to remember for navigating the river of change without getting swamped ...

- Remember to pack your attitude.
- Don't look where you don't want to go.
- Go with the flow.
- Explore what's around the next bend.
- Take time to eddy out.

Life is change.
Growth is Optional.

Slide 7–10

How Do You Communicate?

PREFERRED METHODS OF TAKING IN INFORMATION
(MODALITIES)

MODALITY	AVERAGE
Visual	60 – 72%
Auditory	12 – 18%
Kinesthetic	18 – 30%

Slide 7–11

Coaching

What is reality	What is desired
Facts, no interpretation	Aligned with business, DISC, PIAV
Observable behaviors	Measurable and achievable
Employee's feelings	Desirable by all

Focus on growing talents, not fixing weaknesses.

Slide 7–12

Coaching (continued)

BUSINESS COACHING:

Focus on business change, not personal growth.
"Therapy looks back, coaching looks forward."

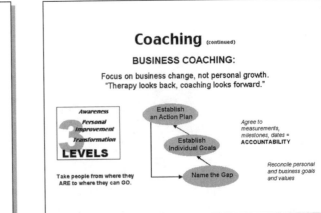

Slide 7–13

Coaching Language

Avoid directing the discussion.
NOT *"No, that's the wrong goal."*

Avoid analysis and interpretation.
NOT *"Yes, I know which part bothers you the most!"*

Phrase future in the present state.
NOT *"What will your relationship be like?"*

Push to the end result, not just next step.
NOT *"Promotion is what you want."*

Slide 7–14

Coaching Language

Questions to help people learn and explore:

- What would happen if you asked for help in this area in which you're not so skilled?
- What's stopping you from requesting a change?
- If you died today, what regrets would you have?
- How might you deal with the conflict without resorting to a win/lose posture?
- Why do you want to lead, and why should people follow you?
- What legacy do you want to leave behind? What do you want people to say about you after you've left your current role?
- What are your vulnerabilities, and where could things fall apart?
- What can you do to renew yourself? Your team? This company?

Slide 7–15

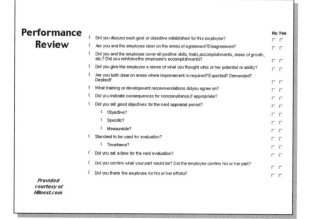

Slide 7–16

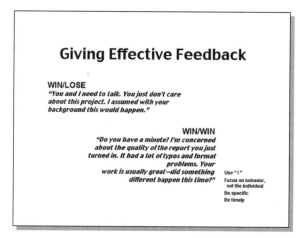

Slide 7–17

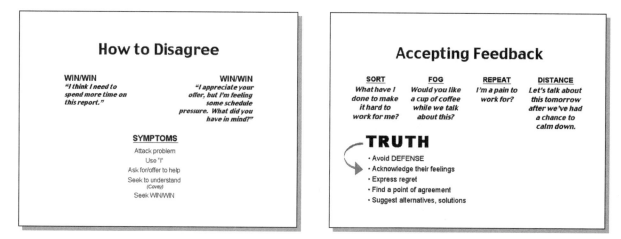

Slide 7–18

Slide 7–19

Feedback Pointers

GIVING	RECEIVING
Be specific,	*Be open,*
descriptive,	*take notes,*
action–oriented,	*ask for examples,*
nonjudgmental	*seek to understand,*
	triangulate information later

Slide 7–20

A Difficult Conversations Checklist

What Happened?
Where does your story come from? Facts? Past Experience? Rules? Theirs?
What impact has this had on you? What might their intentions have been?
What have you contributed to the problem?

Emotions
What are you really feeling? Why?

Identify
What's at stake for you about you?

Purposes
What do you hope to accomplish? Shift to support learning, sharing, problem-solving.
Is this the best way to address this issue?

Differences
Describe the problem in terms of the differences between your stories.
Share your purposes.
Invite them to join as a partner to solve the problem.

Explore the Stories
Listen to understand their perspective.
Share your viewpoint.
Reframe, reframe, reframe to keep on track.

Problem Solving
Invent options that meet each side's concerns.
Look to standards for what should happen.
Talk about how to keep communication open going forward.

Adapted from the book Difficult Conversations by Douglas Stone, Bruce Patton and Sheila Heen.

Slide 7–21

Bibliography

PROJECT MANAGEMENT / LEADERSHIP:

Brooks, F. *The Mythical Man Month.* Addison-Wesley, 1975.

Cougar, J. D. and Zawacki, R. A. "What Motivates DP Professionals?" *Datamation.* September, 1978 pp. 116-123.

DeMarco, T. and Lister, T. *Peopleware: Productive Projects and Teams.* Dorset House, 1986.

England, Randy and Graham. *Creating a Project Environment.* Jossey-Bass, 1997.

Frost, P., Mitchell, V. and Nord, W. *Organizational Reality: Reports from the Firing Line.* Scott, Foresman and Company, 1986.

Hampton, D., Summer, C. and Webber, R. *Organizational Behavior and the Practice of Management.* Scott, Foresman and Company, 1987.

Haynes, Marion E. *Project Management.* Crisp Publications, 1989.

Rakos, John J. *Software Project Management for Small to Medium Sized Projects.* Prentice Hall, 1991.

Roberts, W. *Leadership Secrets of Attila the Hun.* Warner Books, 1987.

Russell, Lou. *The Accelerated Learning Fieldbook: Making the Instructional Process Fast, Flexible, and Fun.* San Francisco: Jossey-Bass Pfeiffer, 1999.

Russell, Lou. *Project Management for Trainers.* Virginia: ASTD, 2000.

Russell, Lou. *IT Leadership Alchemy.* Prentice Hall, 2002.

Thomsett, R. *People and Project Management.* Yourdon Press, 1980.

Weinberg, G. *The Psychology of Computer Programming.* Van Nostrand Reinhold, 1971.

Yourdon, E. *Managing the Structured Techniques.* Yourdon Press, 1979.

◆

Two-Day Program

What's in This Chapter?

- ◆ Objectives for presenting a two-day workshop stressing all 10 leadership competencies

- ◆ Detailed program agenda

- ◆ Criteria for ongoing development after the two-day workshop

The two-day workshop is the most comprehensive facilitation of the leadership material. It spends at least one hour, including an exercise, on each leadership competency. It begins with the learners completing a self-assessment on the 10 leadership competencies and uses DISC (Dominance, Influence, Steadiness, and Compliance) and PIAV (Personal Interests, Attitudes, and Values) assessment profiles. It ends with the learners creating a development action plan.

The material is slightly different from the one-day version, so it would be a good reinforcement if the learners have attended the half-day or one-day program. All three categories of leadership competencies will be covered: Self-Alignment, Working with Others, and Integration.

Two-Day Program

TRAINING OBJECTIVES

The objectives for the two-day leadership training workshop are to

- ◆ understand and apply participants' personal values and leadership style

- ◆ influence and build relationships within and across organizations

- manage change and transition

- lead others with diverse styles

- align actions and priorities with strategic direction

- coach and develop others for motivation and performance.

MATERIALS

For the instructor:

- This chapter for reference

- Learning Activity 10–2: Lead/Manage

- Learning Activity 10–3: Personal Mission

- Learning Activity 10–4: Self-Assessment

- Learning Activity 10–5: Behavioral Style

- Learning Activity 10–6: Resiliency Attitude

- Learning Activity 10–8: Imposing Order on Chaos

- Learning Activity 10–9: Sabotage

- Learning Activity 10–10: Coaching Role Play

- Learning Activity 10–11: Blending Styles

- Learning Activity 10–12: Adapting Styles

- Learning Activity 10–13: Listening

- Learning Activity 10–14: Feedback

- Learning Activity 10–15: Creating a Vision

- Learning Activity 10–16: Customer Orientation

- Learning Activity 10–17: STEM

- Learning Activity 10–18: Remembering

- Learning Activity 10–19: Scenario Planning

- Learning Activity 10–20: Delphi Technique

- Learning Activity 10–21: Nominal Group Technique

- Learning Activity: 10–22: Project Leadership

- Learning Activity 10–23: The Big Close

- Tool 11–1: The Hero's Journey

- Tool 11–2: Systems Thinking

- Tool 11–3: Mini-Evaluation

- Tool 11–4: General Workshop Appraisal

- PowerPoint slides "Everyday Leadership" (slides 1–115 beginning on page 81). To access slides for this program, open the file *Two-Day.ppt* on the accompanying CD. Copies of the slides for this training session are included at the end of this chapter.

For the participants:

- Handout 11–1: The 10 Leadership Competencies

- Handout 11–2: Chuck's Role

- Handout 11–3: Angela's Role

- Handout 11–4: Observation Checklist

- Handout 11–5: A Difficult Conversations Checklist

- Handout 11–6: Adapting Your Style: Working with Core Style D

- Handout 11–7: Adapting Your Style: Working with Core Style I

- Handout 11–8: Adapting Your Style: Working with Core Style S

- Handout 11–9: Adapting Your Style: Working with Core Style C

- Handout 11–10: The Sabotage Exercise

- Handout 11–11: Team Member Assignment Cards for the Sabotage Exercise

- Handout 11–12: Feedback

- Handout 11–13: Hints and Solutions for Feedback

- Handout 11–14: The Hero's Journey

- Handout 11–15: Delphi Technique Case Study

- Assessment 11–1: Leadership Self-Assessment (optional)

- ◆ Assessment 11–2: Quick n' Dirty DISC/PIAV Assessment (optional)

- ◆ Training Instrument 11–2: Identification of Strengths and Weaknesses

- ◆ Training Instrument 11–3: Nine Dots

- ◆ Training Instrument 11–4: Practicing Flexibility: A Test of Your Creative Thinking Skills

- ◆ Training Instrument 11–5: Journaling: Resiliency

- ◆ Training Instrument 11–6: Journaling: Working with Others

- ◆ Training Instrument 11–7: Blending of Styles

- ◆ Training Instrument 11–8: Walk a Mile in My Shoes . . .

- ◆ Training Instrument 11–9: Journaling: Communication

- ◆ Training Instrument 11–10: Performance Review

- ◆ Training Instrument 11–11: Journaling: Coaching

- ◆ Training Instrument 11–12: Journaling: Vision

- ◆ Training Instrument 11–13: Change Versus Transition

- ◆ Training Instrument 11–14: Journaling: Change

- ◆ Training Instrument 11–15: Journaling: Customer Orientation

- ◆ Training Instrument 11–16: Nominal Group Technique Case Study

- ◆ Training Instrument 11–17: Journaling: Strategic Business Acumen

- ◆ Training Instrument 11–18: Document Risk and Constraints

- ◆ Training Instrument 11–19: Journaling: Project Leadership

- ◆ Training Instrument 11–20: Strength Worksheet

- ◆ Training Instrument 11–21: Opportunity Worksheet

- ◆ Training Instrument 11–22: Action Plan

- ◆ three-ring binder for each participant, for handouts and other sheets

- ◆ blank paper for each participant

- ◆ tent cards or name tags for each participant

Using the CD

Materials for this training session are provided in this workbook and as electronic files on the accompanying CD. To access the electronic files, insert the CD and click on the appropriate Adobe .pdf document. Further directions and help in locating and using the files can be found in Appendix A, "Using the Compact Disc."

Sample Agenda: First Day

8:00 a.m. Welcome (10 minutes)

Show the slide 8–1 as participants enter. When they are all seated, show the "Course Contents" slide (slide 8–2). Explain that this session will explore competencies and beliefs about participants' own leadership roles. Emphasize that the goal is to identify unique strengths so they can be leveraged in the unique leadership role of each individual. Also explain that the tendency will be to focus on the weaknesses or gaps, but these will only be explored in order to grow them to a "good enough," minimal competency. In other words, the idea is to "strengthen the hands of the strong" versus turning everyone into clones.

As facilitator, you will have to work very diligently at keeping the focus away from "how flawed I am."

Show slide 8–3. Ask participants to silently pick their top objective. Read through the list again and ask for a show of hands, noting which objectives are the most desired. This will give you a sense of what material can be discussed more quickly and which sections need a bit more time. Each time you teach this workshop it will be slightly different.

8:10 Critical Leadership (10 minutes)

Refer learners to slide 8–4 to introduce the first unit. Use slides 8–5 and 8–6 to lead learners through a discussion about why leadership is so critical now and so often missing. Ask for their feedback and thoughts.

8:20   Learning Activity 10–2: Lead/Manage (chapter 10, page 110) (20 minutes)

Conduct this activity, which introduces the participants to the concept of leadership and shows them the difference between leading and managing.

8:40   Learning Activity: 10–3: Personal Mission (chapter 10, page 112) (20 minutes)

In this exercise, participants will work alone to come up with three nouns and a verb to describe their personal missions. Help them to understand that a personal mission is a statement of why they are on Earth.

Ask the participants to introduce themselves (with job and company if appropriate) and share a phrase that states their personal missions. This works best if you go first, sharing your own personal mission statement. Ask them to write their phrases on the front of their name tent cards.

9:00   Break (15 minutes)

9:15   Self-Assessment (20 minutes)

Show PowerPoint slide 8–11. You are now going to go over the 360–degree assessments to help people understand themselves as leaders. It is strongly recommended that full assessments be used at this point.

If you are licensing the use of full assessments, you will have asked the participants to complete them before they came to class and, at this point, will ask them to take out their reports. If you did not do assessments before the class, distribute Assessment 11–1: Leadership Self-Assessment (chapter 11, page 169) and conduct Learning Activity 10–4: Self-Assessment (chapter 10, page 114).

9:20   Behavioral Style (20 minutes)

If you did not license full assessments distribute Assessment 11–2: Quick n' Dirty DISC/PIAV Assessment and conduct Learning Activity 10–5: Behavioral Style (chapter 10, page 115). The DISC (Dominance, Influence, Steadiness, and Compliance) Assessment is a nonscientific way to determine how each learner behaves and how others would describe the behavior. The PIAV (Personal Interests, Attitudes, and Values) Assessment helps determine what appeals to each learner and what he or she avoids.

9:55   Break (20 minutes)

10:15   Leadership Competencies (30 minutes)

Now it is time to return to the competencies, using slide 8–18. Remember, the participants have already read through the competencies. Ask them to take out the results of the 360–degree assessments they completed before class to refer to as the class goes along. If they did not complete assessments before the session they can refer to Assessment 11–1.

Ask learners to finish up by reflecting on the questions on Training Instrument 11–2: Identification of Strengths and Weaknesses (chapter 11, page 180). At the end of each unit through the rest of the program there will be a journaling handout, similar to this, that the participants can use to help them think about different aspects of their lives and record their thoughts. It is important that you allow plenty of reflective time in this workshop because of this. Consider passing out the three-ring binders at this point so the participants can organize their different assessments and journal entries through the rest of the course.

10:45   Introducing Resiliency (10 minutes)

Show slides 8–19 and 8–20 to introduce the competency of Resiliency. Show slide 8–21 and explain that this section deals with learning to weather change well. Tell the learners that material to come will help them to lead others through change, but that the Resiliency competency is focused on them as leaders. Explain that you will now walk through the five traits of resiliency:

◆ building the resiliency attitude

◆ looking into the future

- practicing flexibility

- imposing order on chaos

- seeking opportunities in change.

10:55　Learning Activity 10–6: Resiliency Attitude (chapter 10, page 119) (5 minutes)

Give each person a blank piece of paper and conduct this learning activity. Use slide 8–22 to talk about a resilient attitude and encourage learners to share their own stories about when they were able to be resilient.

11:00　Looking into the Future (5 minutes)

Discuss slide 8–23 and ask the participants to share their thoughts or encourage them to jot down a couple of their thoughts.

11:05　Flexible Thinking (10 minutes)

Pass out Training Instrument 11–3: Nine Dots (chapter 11, page 181). Tell the participants that the goal is to connect all the dots without lifting the pen from the paper. Someone in your class probably knows the answer to this, so ask for volunteers to share the answer on a flipchart. Explain how thinking past the obvious helps with resiliency. Pass out Training Instrument 11–4: Practicing Flexibility (chapter 11, page 182) show slide 8–24, and have people raise their hands if they know the answer to each question. Point out that the answers depend on looking past what the questions are asking in the literal sense.

11:15　Learning Activity 10–8: Imposing Order on Chaos (chapter 10, page 123) (5 minutes)

Show slide 8–25 and conduct this activity.

11:20　Seeking Opportunities (10 minutes)

Discuss slide 8–26 and then discuss the questions on slide 8–27 as a group. Summarize this unit of the session with slide 8–28 and pass out Training Instrument 11–5:

Journaling: Resiliency (chapter 11, page 184) so the learners can reflect on their own resiliency.

11:30   Lunch (90 minutes)

1:00 p.m.   Interpersonal and Relationship Skills (30 minutes)

Using slides 8–29 and 8–30, introduce the competency of Interpersonal and Relationship Skills. Then conduct Learning Activity 10–9: Sabotage (chapter 10, page 124). You will be able to apply the experience of this great exercise (written by Thiagi, www.thiagi.com) through the next couple of sections.

1:30   Trustworthiness (10 minutes)

Discuss slide 8–31, referring to the Sabotage exercise. Ask people to raise their hands if they are trustworthy. Of course every person will raise his or her hand. Ask the participants: If everyone in trustworthy, then why is there a problem with trust? Talk about the components of trust (credibility, consistency, and communication). Ask people to think about the questions on slide 8–32 and then share their thoughts about trust, which is an important part of leadership.

1:40   Broken Trust (10 minutes)

Trust can be broken simply and accidentally by the language we use. Have learners look at slide 8–33 and ask for a volunteer to explain which words actually make the difference. Emphasize the following:

    •   Stick to facts and avoid emotion and interpretation ("Example: You don't care about this project . . . ").

    •   Use "I" rather than "You."

1:50   Break (15 minutes)

2:05   Learning Activity 10–10: Coaching Role Play (chapter 10, page 126) (30 minutes)

This exercise will draw on all that the learners have done so far today.

2:35　　Role Play Conflict (10 minutes)

Use slide 8–34 to point out where conflict occurred in the role play. Use slide 8–35 and Handout 11–5: A Difficult Conversations Checklist (chapter 11, pages 153) to re-emphasize some tips for more effective difficult conversations. Use Training Instrument 11–6: Journaling: Working with Others (chapter 11, page 185) to finish up the discussion of this competency and to encourage your learners to take a few minutes to reflect on what they've learned through these exercises and discussions.

2:45　　Communication Skills (10 minutes)

Introduce the next competency of Communication Skills, using slides 8–36 and 8–37. The next material will focus on how the participants can adapt their communication styles to that of other people and will use the DISC/PIAV profiles discussed in the morning. Again, if you prefer to use a different kind of profile, please substitute your own slides for slides 8–40 through 8–44.

2:55　　What Is Said Versus What Is Heard (10 minutes)

Call the learners' attention to the question at the top of slide 8–38. Ask one of the learners to read the question out loud in each of the following ways:

◆　as if he or she was asking out of curiosity

◆　as if the person being asked had just done something really stupid

◆　as if the person being asked was the wrong person to do that task.

Ask for volunteers to explain the concepts of Message (what you said—the words), Channels (how it was communicated—spoken, demonstrated, email—in this case the emphasis was on different words, depending on the context), and Interference (the things that block understanding—such as word use, historical relationship, confusion at the time). Ask for examples of breakdowns in each case. Explain that what is said is rarely the most influential and point out the percentages at the bottom of the slide.

3:05   Presentation Skills (5 minutes)

Discuss the model for presentation skills on slide 8–39. Ask each person to silently reflect on the part of his or her presentation approach that is strongest and the part that is weakest. Ask them to set some goals for future improvement in this area as you release them for a break.

3:10   Break (15 minutes)

3:25   Natural Styles (5 minutes)

If you used the licensed assessments, ask learners to look at their adapted DISC profiles. The page in their profiles should look like that on slide 8–40, which is a sample. Using this slide, explain that everyone must adapt situationally to get along well with others but that the more people adapt by crossing above or below the main energy line on a regular basis—for example, to fit into a job that is not the best job for their natural style—the more stress they are under. Adaptation is better as temporary change than as a lifestyle.

3:30   Learning Activity 10–11: Blending Styles (chapter 10, page 128) (15 minutes)

Conduct this learning activity, which shows different characteristics of the DISC profiles.

3:45   Learning Activity 10:12 Adapting Styles (chapter 10, page 130) (20 minutes)

Ask learners to read the instructions on slides 8–41 through 8–44 (Handouts 11–6 through 11–9, chapter 11, pages 154–157) for adapting to the style they have chosen. This activity will help learners practice adapting behavioral styles.

4:05   Listening (5 minutes)

Read through slide 8–45 with the learners. Refer to the material from the earlier section covering trust. Discuss the concept of asking genuine questions—you truly want to know and are interested. Non-genuine questions include talking so people notice you (that's about you, not them), or asking questions to trip up the other person, or just talking to fill the silence but not to add value. Continue with slide 8–46 on reflective listening—refer to the conflict in the earlier unit—use "I" rather than "shoulds" or "coulds."

4:10   Learning Activity 10–13: Listening (chapter 10, page 131) (10 minutes)

This activity helps learners understand how to listen in a reflective manner.

4:20   Assign Training Instrument 11–9: Journaling: Communication (chapter 11, pages 188) as homework for the next day. Ask the participants to review all their journal pages before the next session.

Sample Agenda: Second Day

Lead learners through slides 8–47 and 8–48 briefly, as you did with all the other competencies. Then begin the session with an exercise.

8:00 a.m.   Learning Activity 10–14: Feedback (chapter 10, page 132) (30 minutes)

Look at the learning activity notes to see how to distribute the handouts for this activity correctly, which is critical to the exercise's success. This fun exercise is based on a frame game developed by Thiagi (www.thiagi.com) to help learners begin to think about communication, leadership, coaching, and feedback. The debriefing from this exercise can be leveraged the rest of the day.

8:30   Therapy Versus Coaching (5 minutes)

Use slide 8–49 and the results of the last learning activity to emphasize the difference between therapy and coaching—therapy goes back, coaching goes forward. Explain that the flow of coaching is to establish a gap in abilities, establish goals for closing the gap, and work on implementing an action plan. Explain that the coach's role is to be a mirror—facilitating the direction that is being discovered by the person being coached.

8:35   Goals (5 minutes)

Read through slide 8–50. Emphasize the difference between a business goal and a personal goal, referring often to the results of the Feedback exercise and the lessons learned from it. Show slide 8–51 and point out that in coaching personal goals are established through helping the coached person see the gaps he or she wants to bridge. Also stress the coaching "maturity" levels: Is the person being coached at the point of needing self-awareness (to see the gaps), performance improvement (set and move toward goal improvement), or transformation (adopt a completely new personal mission)? Finish by talking through the coaching process on slide 8–52, starting at the stage of Determine What Needs to Happen.

8:40   Coaching Language (5 minutes)

Showing slide 8–53, ask for volunteers to restate the "not" phrases in better coaching language. Read through the list of good coaching questions on slide 8–54. Ask the participants to pick their favorite and vote with a show of hands.

8:45   Coaching for Performance Reviews (15 minutes)

Slide 8–55 deals with holding effective performance reviews, a common competency gap for leaders. Distribute Training Instrument 11–10: Performance Review (chapter 11, page 189) and ask the learners to put stars next to the actions they already do well and to circle three they would like to adopt. Have volunteers share some of what they marked with the others.

9:00   Effective Feedback (10 minutes)

Slide 8–56 was already used in the first day—show it here to review good "I" language, which also is critical to coaching success. Slide 8–57 shows two "win/win" state-

ments, with some review points about good coaching and conflict resolution language.

9:10   Accepting Feedback (15 minutes)

Slide 8–58 shows how a coach can respond if he or she is taken aback by feedback from someone being coached. When someone has insulted or confronted you in a coaching session, these are the best techniques for getting enough time to get your response and your emotions under control.

To practice, say to the learners, "You are impossible to work with and your clothes are ugly!" Ask for five volunteers to respond in a Sort, Fog, Repeat, and Distance manner. Review slide 8–59 and share ideas as a group for taking, receiving, and giving feedback more effectively. Pass out Training Instrument 11–11: Journaling: Coaching (chapter 11, page 190) and ask learners to spend a few minutes on it before going on break.

9:25   Break (15 minutes)

9:40   Learning Activity 10–15: Creating a Vision (chapter 10, page 134) (15 minutes)

This introduces the competency of Creating Vision, using slides 8–60 and 8–61.

9:55   Contributing to the Vision (20 minutes)

Using the team or organizational vision, ask learners to make a list of 10 things they do during a typical day. Have the learners use the directions on slide 8–62 to prioritize these tasks. Explain that most of the 360-degree assessments list this as their biggest need—they know the vision, but they want to know how to contribute. Discuss any misunderstandings or challenges. Have each participant use slide 8–63 to create three measurable goals based on the vision for the business that they created. Emphasize that in a business, the performance goals must contribute to the business goals Improve Revenue, Avoid Cost, and Improve Service (IRACIS) and align with the organization's vision. Have participants reflect for several minutes on the questions on Training Instrument 11–12: Journaling: Vision (chapter 11, page 190).

10:15   Break (15 minutes)

10:30   Managing Change (10 minutes)

Introduce the competency of Managing Change using slides 8–64 and 8–65. The earlier unit on Resiliency was directed at the leaders themselves, but this unit focuses on how they can help other people through chance. Begin by asking people to follow the instructions in Training Instrument 11–13: Change Versus Transition (chapter 11, page 192). Using slide 8–66, debrief the group by emphasizing that Change is what happens to us—it is external—but Transition is how we choose to react to the change. This is an important concept to share with the teams you lead. Share the quotation on slide 8–67.

10:40   Phases of Change (10 minutes)

Review slides 8–68 and 8–69 with the learners. This is William Bridges' change model from his book *Managing Transitions.* The model helps people begin to think about the phases of change. Bridges believes that we all go through these three phases in order to be successful at transition:

- ◆   **Endings:** This phase is a mourning phase and requires acknowledgment of loss in order to move on.

- ◆   **Neutral Zone:** As it was on *Star Trek,* this is an unsafe place. When here, you feel as if you are lost and need to get out, but many people can't bring themselves to move forward. Unable to go back, they find themselves stuck here forever.

- ◆   **New Beginning:** Moving into this phase requires acknowledgment of possibilities and opportunities.

10:50   Phases of Transition (10 minutes)

Slide 8–70 shows the emotions associated with the three phases of transition. It is important to remind the participants that people do not always go through these phases or emotions in a linear way—at any time they might move backward or forward.

Ask the learners to think about a major change that has affected their team and imagine where different people might be in the change journey. Pass out Training Instrument 11–14: Journaling: Change (chapter 11, page 193) so they can begin to make notes about the specific changes with which their team is currently grappling.

11:00　The Hero's Journey (25 minutes)

Explain that Bridges speaks from a linear model, but that transition is generally more a case of two steps forward, one step back. Contrast that to slide 8–71, which shows The Hero's Journey by Joseph Campbell. This model emphasizes that we are all heroes, constantly dealing with change and in transition. Distribute Handout 11–14: The Hero's Journey (chapter 11, page 163), briefly explain the model (learning about it from Tool 11–1: The Hero's Journey, chapter 11, page 203), and then use a widely known fairy tale (the tool uses Sleeping Beauty) to illustrate the different phases. Ask the participants to relate the questions on slide 8–72 to a business-related transition they have made.

11:25　Learning Activity 10–16: Customer Orientation (chapter 10, page 135) (15 minutes)

Conduct this activity before breaking for lunch.

11:40　Consulting Focus (15 minutes)

Slide 8–77 emphasizes the difference between a product focus and a consulting focus, and slide 8–78 shares phrases to avoid. Leaders must promote a customer focus with their teams. Slides 8–79 emphasizes that each business competes along different dimensions (based on Michael Treacy and Fred Wiersema's book *The Discipline of Market Leaders*). Point out that a company can differentiate itself by being the least expensive, quickest to market, or most customer intimate (this is more than customer service—it requires shared risk with the customer). Ask each learner to reflect on which one his or her company is striving to be and ask for a show of hands for each. Point out that the same differentiator must, through their leadership, also drive their teams. Give learners five minutes to document their customer, their product, their competition, and how they differentiate. Have volunteers share some of their answers. Show slides 8–80 and 8–81, which talk specifically about identifying what the customer really needs (versus wants) and separating causes from symptoms.

11:55   Lunch (65 minutes)

1:00 p.m.   Conduct Learning Activity 11–17: STEM (chapter 10, page 136) (10 minutes)

This activity helps participants separate symptoms from causes.

1:10   Customer Presentations (20 minutes)

Use slide 8–83 to make the transition into a discussion on customer presentations and meetings. Emphasize the wide variety of options available.

1:30   Learning Activity 10–18: Remembering (chapter 10, page 137) (20 minutes)

This activity shows participants factors that influence memory and how to help people improve their ability to retain information.

1:50   What's in It for Me? (15 minutes)

Use slides 8–87 and 8–88 to emphasize the importance of customer service orientation. WIIFM stands for What's in It for Me? and refers to why the customer should do business with you. Emphasize that an unhappy customer tells more people about their experience than a happy customer and discuss the other elements noted on the slide. Pass out Training Instrument 11–15: Journaling:

Customer Orientation (chapter 11, page 194) and ask people to log their thoughts before break.

2:05   Break (20 minutes)

2:25   Strategic Business Acumen (15 minutes)

Use slides 8–89 and 8–90 to introduce Strategic Business Acumen. It is critical that a leader understands the business and helps the team understand it. This unit will quickly introduce two learning organization techniques, Systems Thinking and Scenario Planning, and three group consensus techniques, the Brainstorming, Delphi, and Nominal Group techniques. This is meant to be an overview only and is in no way an adequate exposure to any of these topics. The Resources section lists other resources for future exploration if you or the learners are interested.

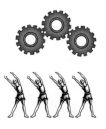

If you are not comfortable with the concept of Systems Thinking, I recommend that you remove slides 8–91 and 8–92. Otherwise, use Training Tool 11–2 (chapter 11, page 205) to explain Systems Thinking.

2:40   Learning Activity 10–19: Scenario Planning (chapter 10, page 139) (15 minutes)

This activity introduces the concept of planning for alternate futures.

2:55   Group Consensus Techniques (10 minutes)

Finish this unit by demonstrating the group techniques introduced on slide 8–96. If you are short on time, explain how to use each technique, using slides 8–97 through 8–101. If you have time, you can try each technique, or one or two of them.

Slide 8–97 deals with Group Creativity and Group Think. When gathering information from a group of people, you must manage the tension between these two things. Research has proven that groups tend to be more creative than single individuals (Group Creativity). However, individuals in groups tend to be influenced by others to be-

have in ways that differ from how they would behave as individuals (Group Think). Point out that, as leaders, the participants need to ensure that these elements stay in balance when dealing with a group of people. Slides 8–98 and 8–99 describe brainstorming. Ask teams to brainstorm a good metaphor for leadership (for example, horticulture—you plant lots of stuff, but you can never be sure what grows). Give each team two minutes to generate as many unique ideas as possible. Reward the winning team. Point out that this technique is useful for creativity, but is not good for consensus building or convergence of opinions.

3:05   Break (15 minutes)

3:20   Learning Activity 10–20: Delphi Technique (chapter 10, page 140) (10 minutes)

This activity introduces the Delphi Technique of reaching group conclusions.

3:30   Learning Activity 10–21: Nominal Group Technique (chapter 10, page 141) (10 minutes)

This is useful when a meeting has fallen apart or you think there will be a great deal of conflict.

3:40   Ask learners to take five minutes and use Training Instrument 11–17: Journaling: Strategic Business Acumen (chapter 11, page 196) to reflect on their strategic business acumen.

3:45   Learning Activity 10–22: Project Leadership (chapter 10, page 142) (20 minutes)

This activity introduces the learners to the concepts of planning projects and assessing the risks and constraints associated with them.

4:05   Ask learners to take five minutes to journal using Training Instrument 11–19: Journaling: Project Leadership (chapter 11, page 198).

4:10   Action Plans (10 minutes)

Invite the learners to read each of the journaling pages in all the units. Pass out Training Instrument 11–20: Strength Worksheet; Training Instrument 11–21: Opportunity Worksheet; Training Instrument 11–22: Action Plan; and Handout 11–14: The Hero's Journey (all in chapter 11). Point learners to slides 8–113 through 8–115 for samples of action plans based on strengths and opportunities. If you have time, you can allow people to begin this in class, but it also can be done on their own. Always give them a few minutes to write down at least one action they'd like to take.

After they have done this, toss a Koosh ball around and ask each person to share one thing they've learned about leadership. Safety rules: make eye contact, say person's name, toss underhand.

4:20 p.m. After distributing evaluations (use Tools 11–3 and 11–4 in chapter 11, if you wish) and diplomas, finish with Learning Activity 10–23: The Big Close (chapter 10, page 144).

What to Do Next

◆ Using the material in chapter 2 as a guide, build a detailed plan to prepare for this session, including schedule and room reservations, invitations, supply list, teaching notes, and time estimate.

◆ Plan how to implement an Action Plan for the learners, using chapter 9 as a guide.

◆ Implement these plans.

◆ Evaluate the effectiveness of the program, using the ideas presented in chapter 4.

◆ Consider follow-up sessions or "alumni" meetings to encourage learners in their leadership journeys.

Slide 8–1

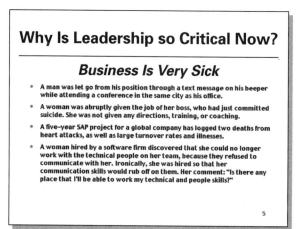

EVERYDAY LEADERSHIP

by
YOUR NAME HERE
YOUR CONTACT INFO

Slide 8–2

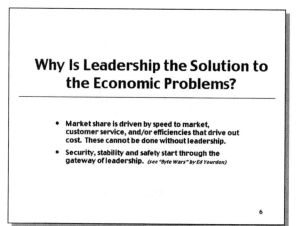

Course Contents

STRENGTHEN THE
HANDS OF THE
STRONG

Unit 1: Overview – Why is leadership so critical now?

Unit 2: Self Alignment: Awareness of the 10 Competencies

Unit 3: Self Alignment: Resiliency

Unit 4: Working With Others: Interpersonal and Relationship Skills

Unit 5: Communication Skills

Unit 6: Employee Development/Coaching

Unit 7: Creating Vision

Unit 8: Change

Unit 9: Integration: Customer Orientation

Unit 10: Business Acumen

Unit 11: Project Leadership

2

Slide 8–3

Course Objectives

After completing this workshop, the learner will be able to:

- Understand and apply their personal values and leadership style.
- Influence and build relationships within and across organizations.
- Manage change and transition.
- Lead others with diverse styles.
- Align actions and priorities with strategic direction.
- Coach and develop others for motivation and performance.

3

Slide 8–4

Overview:
Why Is Leadership so Critical Now?

- Companies are very sick

- What is Management? Leadership?

"In the Land of the Blind, One–Eyed Men Are Kings." – French Proverb

4

Slide 8–5

Why Is Leadership so Critical Now?

Business Is Very Sick

- A man was let go from his position through a text message on his beeper while attending a conference in the same city as his office.
- A woman was abruptly given the job of her boss, who had just committed suicide. She was not given any directions, training, or coaching.
- A five–year SAP project for a global company has logged two deaths from heart attacks, as well as large turnover rates and illnesses.
- A woman hired by a software firm discovered that she could no longer work with the technical people on her team, because they refused to communicate with her. Ironically, she was hired so that her communication skills would rub off on them. Her comment: "Is there any place that I'll be able to work my technical and people skills?"

5

Slide 8–6

Why Is Leadership the Solution to the Economic Problems?

- Market share is driven by speed to market, customer service, and/or efficiencies that drive out cost. These cannot be done without leadership.
- Security, stability and safety start through the gateway of leadership. *(see "Byte Wars" by Ed Yourdon)*

6

Slide 8–7

What Is Management? Leadership?

LEAD   **MANAGE**

7

Slide 8–8

How Is Leadership Unique?

- The "why" of a business, organization or team is critical for project / resource prioritization but generally **unknown**.
- Leadership development is a paradox. It must be practical and immediate. However, to be able to "do," leaders must find quiet time to develop self-understanding. There is a strong tension between the need to act quickly and the need to stop and think. Leadership requires **both**.

8

Slide 8–9

A Great Leader

- A great leader needs to know how to leverage the strengths she already has, and to surround herself with others to fill in her own gaps.
- A great leader realizes that each of his people is unique and coaches them to leverage their own strengths.
- Therefore, leadership is about releasing the potential that is already there.

9

Slide 8–10

What Is Management? Leadership?

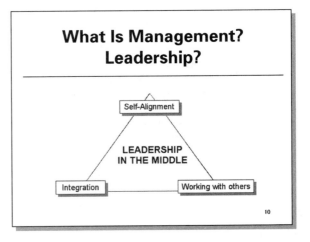

Self-Alignment

LEADERSHIP
IN THE MIDDLE

Integration   Working with others

10

Slide 8–11

Self-Understanding: Self-Assessment

- Definition of the Competency
- Self-Assessment
- 360-Degree Assessment
- Identification of Strengths and Weaknesses

"To climb a tree, grab the branches not the blossoms. " –Unknown

11

Slide 8–12

The DISC & PIAV

MOTIVATORS
Why and *Where* you walk

BEHAVIOR
How you are walking?

- No Right or Wrong Profile
- No Good or Bad Profile
- Does not measure
  - Intelligence
  - Ethics
  - Skill or ability

12

Slide 8–13

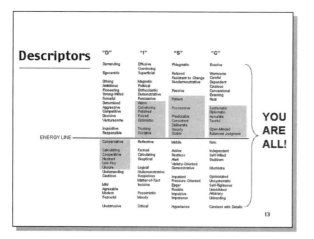

Slide 8–14

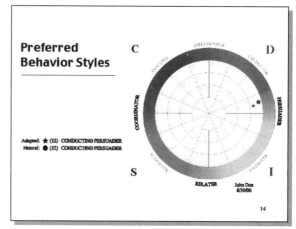

Slide 8–15

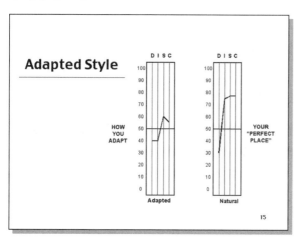

Slide 8–16

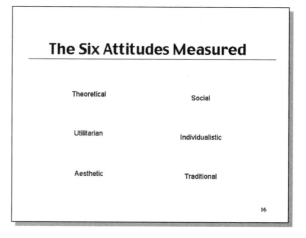

Slide 8–17

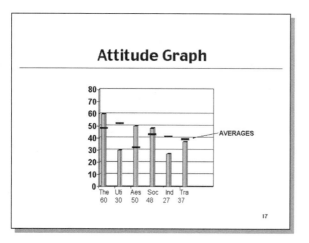

Slide 8–18

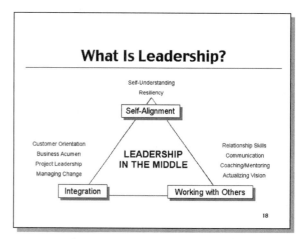

Slide 8–19

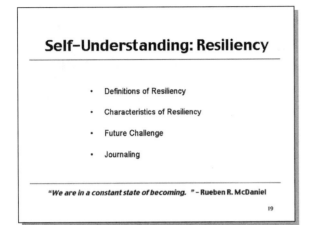

Slide 8–20

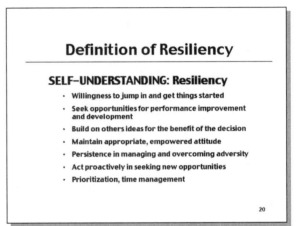

Slide 8–21

Slide 8–22

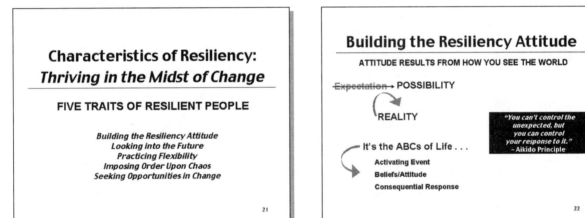

Slide 8–23

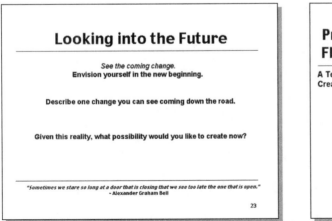

Slide 8–24

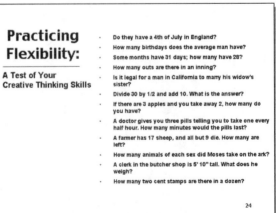

Slide 8–25

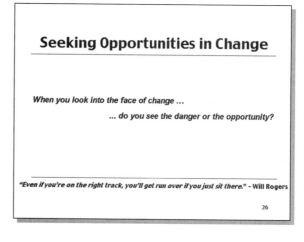

Imposing Order upon Chaos

Take First Things First

You are driving down a lonely stretch of highway late one night when you come upon an accident. A car is overturned on the road. A second car with a smashed front end sits sideways halfway onto the shoulder. You see small flames beginning to flicker up from under this car's hood. A wounded deer lies not far from the first car. As you pull up to the scene and prepare to stop, your headlights shine on a person in the overturned vehicle. You can see that he is halfway out of the car and bleeding badly from a gash in his forehead. Glancing quickly at the other vehicle, you see a person moving slightly in the driver's seat. The back door of this car is open and there is a small child standing by the driver's door. You are alone. You have a cell phone. There is no other traffic on the road.

What are the first five actions you take?

"The law of nature is change (chaos), while the dream of man is order." – Henry Adams

25

Slide 8–26

Seeking Opportunities in Change

When you look into the face of change ...

... do you see the danger or the opportunity?

"Even if you're on the right track, you'll get run over if you just sit there." – Will Rogers

26

Slide 8–27

Future Change

Think of a big change that you think may be ahead of you. What are your strategies for planning how you will personally deal with it?

How will you help your team address it?

27

Slide 8–28

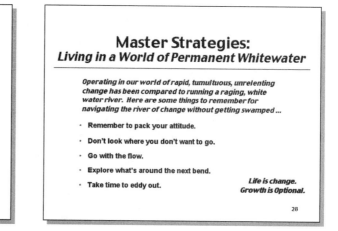

Master Strategies:
Living in a World of Permanent Whitewater

Operating in our world of rapid, tumultuous, unrelenting change has been compared to running a raging, white water river. Here are some things to remember for navigating the river of change without getting swamped ...

- **Remember to pack your attitude.**
- **Don't look where you don't want to go.**
- **Go with the flow.**
- **Explore what's around the next bend.**
- **Take time to eddy out.**

Life is change.
Growth is Optional.

28

Slide 8–29

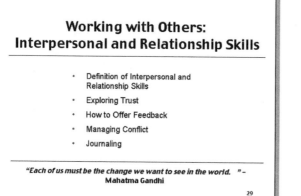

Working with Others:
Interpersonal and Relationship Skills

- Definition of Interpersonal and Relationship Skills
- Exploring Trust
- How to Offer Feedback
- Managing Conflict
- Journaling

"Each of us must be the change we want to see in the world. " –
Mahatma Gandhi

29

Slide 8–30

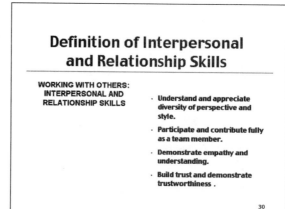

Definition of Interpersonal and Relationship Skills

WORKING WITH OTHERS: INTERPERSONAL AND RELATIONSHIP SKILLS

- **Understand and appreciate diversity of perspective and style.**
- **Participate and contribute fully as a team member.**
- **Demonstrate empathy and understanding.**
- **Build trust and demonstrate trustworthiness .**

30

Slide 8–31

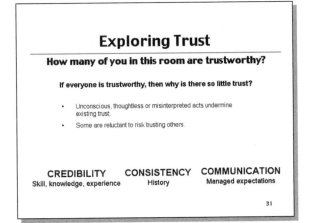

Exploring Trust

How many of you in this room are trustworthy?

If everyone is trustworthy, then why is there so little trust?

- Unconscious, thoughtless or misinterpreted acts undermine existing trust.
- Some are reluctant to risk trusting others.

CREDIBILITY   **CONSISTENCY**   **COMMUNICATION**
Skill, knowledge, experience   History   Managed expectations

31

Slide 8–32

Trust Assessment

SELF-ASSESSMENT:

As a leader, how do you deliver on the three factors that inspire trust?

- What level of credibility do you hold in the context of your leadership role?
- How consistent are you in your actions and decision-making processes?
- How well do you use communication to build confidence and reassurance within your team?

32

Slide 8–33

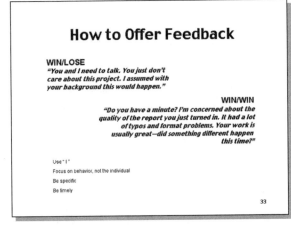

How to Offer Feedback

WIN/LOSE
"You and I need to talk. You just don't care about this project. I assumed with your background this would happen."

WIN/WIN
"Do you have a minute? I'm concerned about the quality of the report you just turned in. It had a lot of typos and format problems. Your work is usually great—did something different happen this time?"

Use "I"
Focus on behavior, not the individual
Be specific
Be timely

33

Slide 8–34

Conflict Situations

SITUATION	EXAMPLE
ambiguous boundaries	_____
conflicting interests	_____
value differences	_____
communication barriers	_____
unresolved prior conflict	_____

TRUST is BIDIRECTIONAL!

34

Slide 8–35

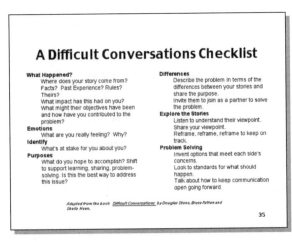

A Difficult Conversations Checklist

What Happened?
Where does your story come from? Facts? Past Experience? Rules? Theirs?
What impact has this had on you?
What might their objectives have been and how have you contributed to the problem?

Emotions
What are you really feeling? Why?

Identify
What's at stake for you about you?

Purposes
What do you hope to accomplish? Shift to support learning, sharing, problem-solving. Is this the best way to address this issue?

Differences
Describe the problem in terms of the differences between your stories and share the purpose.
Invite them to join as a partner to solve the problem.

Explore the Stories
Listen to understand their viewpoint.
Share your viewpoint.
Reframe, reframe, reframe to keep on track.

Problem Solving
Invent options that meet each side's concerns.
Look to standards for what should happen.
Talk about how to keep communication open going forward.

Adapted from the book Difficult Conversations by Douglas Stone, Bruce Patton and Sheila Heen.

35

Slide 8–36

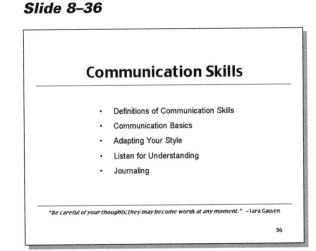

Communication Skills

- Definitions of Communication Skills
- Communication Basics
- Adapting Your Style
- Listen for Understanding
- Journaling

"Be careful of your thoughts; they may become words at any moment." – Iara Gassen

36

Slide 8–37

Definition of Communication Skills

WORKING WITH OTHERS:
Communication Skills

- Understand and adapt to your audience — helping others learn
- Express intention clearly and concisely in written communications
- Build collaboration and clearly articulate intention in verbal communications
- Formal presentation skills
- Listen for understanding
- Manage flow of communication/information

37

Slide 8–38

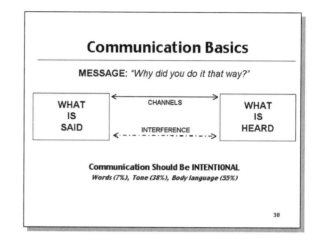

Communication Basics

MESSAGE: *"Why did you do it that way?"*

WHAT IS SAID — CHANNELS / INTERFERENCE — WHAT IS HEARD

Communication Should Be INTENTIONAL
Words (7%), Tone (38%), Body language (55%)

38

Slide 8–39

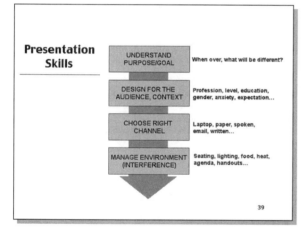

Presentation Skills

UNDERSTAND PURPOSE/GOAL	When over, what will be different?
DESIGN FOR THE AUDIENCE, CONTEXT	Profession, level, education, gender, anxiety, expectation...
CHOOSE RIGHT CHANNEL	Laptop, paper, spoken, email, written...
MANAGE ENVIRONMENT (INTERFERENCE)	Seating, lighting, food, heat, agenda, handouts...

39

Slide 8–40

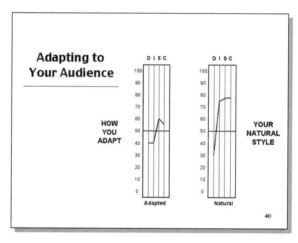

Adapting to Your Audience

HOW YOU ADAPT — DISC — Adapted

YOUR NATURAL STYLE — DISC — Natural

40

Slide 8–41

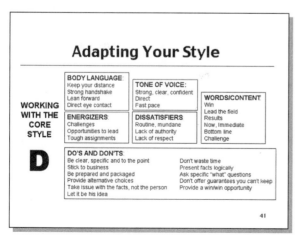

Adapting Your Style

WORKING WITH THE CORE STYLE

BODY LANGUAGE:
Keep your distance
Strong handshake
Lean forward
Direct eye contact

TONE OF VOICE:
Strong, clear, confident
Direct
Fast pace

WORDS/CONTENT:
Win
Lead the field
Results
Now, Immediate
Bottom line
Challenge

ENERGIZERS:
Challenges
Opportunities to lead
Tough assignments

DISSATISFIERS:
Routine, mundane
Lack of authority
Lack of respect

D

DO'S AND DON'TS:
Be clear, specific and to the point
Stick to business
Be prepared and packaged
Provide alternative choices
Take Issue with the facts, not the person
Let it be his idea

Don't waste time
Present facts logically
Ask specific "what" questions
Don't offer guarantees you can't keep
Provide a win/win opportunity

41

Slide 8–42

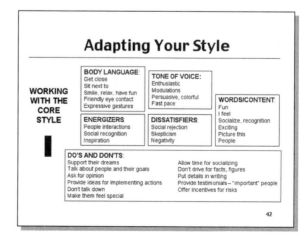

Adapting Your Style

WORKING WITH THE CORE STYLE

BODY LANGUAGE:
Get close
Sit next to
Smile, relax, have fun
Friendly eye contact
Expressive gestures

TONE OF VOICE:
Enthusiastic
Modulations
Persuasive, colorful
Fast pace

WORDS/CONTENT:
Fun
I feel
Socialize, recognition
Exciting
Picture this
People

ENERGIZERS:
People interactions
Social recognition
Inspiration

DISSATISFIERS:
Social rejection
Skepticism
Negativity

I

DO'S AND DON'TS:
Support their dreams
Talk about people and their goals
Ask for opinion
Provide ideas for implementing actions
Don't talk down
Make them feel special

Allow time for socializing
Don't drive for facts, figures
Put details in writing
Provide testimonials – "important" people
Offer incentives for risks

42

Slide 8–43

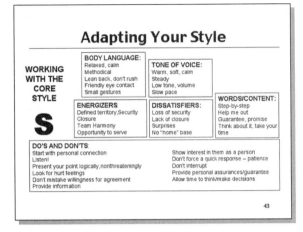

Adapting Your Style

WORKING WITH THE CORE STYLE S

BODY LANGUAGE:
Relaxed, calm
Methodical
Lean back, don't rush
Friendly eye contact
Small gestures

TONE OF VOICE:
Warm, soft, calm
Steady
Low tone, volume
Slow pace

ENERGIZERS
Defined territory,Security
Closure
Team Harmony
Opportunity to serve

DISSATISFIERS:
Loss of security
Lack of closure
Surprises
No "home" base

WORDS/CONTENT:
Step-by-step
Help me out
Guarantee, promise
Think about it, take your time

DO'S AND DON'TS:
Start with personal connection
Listen!
Present your point logically,nonthreateningly
Look for hurt feelings
Don't mistake willingness for agreement
Provide information

Show interest in them as a person
Don't force a quick response – patience
Don't interrupt
Provide personal assurances/guarantee
Allow time to think/make decisions

43

Slide 8–44

Adapting Your Style

WORKING WITH THE CORE STYLE C

BODY LANGUAGE:
Keep your distance
Sit across from
Firm posture
Direct eye contact
Little/no hand gestures

TONE OF VOICE:
Controlled, direct
Thoughtful, precise
Little modulations
Slow pace

WORDS/CONTENT:
Here are the facts
The data show
Proven
Take your time, no risk
Analyze
Guarantees

ENERGIZERS:
Information
Quality Standards
Compliance to rules
Analysis, research

DISSATISFIERS:
Personal criticism
Moving too fast
Decisions without data
Irrational feelings/emotions

DO'S AND DON'TS:
Prepare your case
Approach in straightforward way
Provide policies/rules to follow
Give time for decisions
Be conservative, don't over promise
Prove with facts
Loyalty

Don't be disorganized
Don't be casual, informal or personal
Build credibility – look at all sides
Present specifics
Take time, but be persistent
Help them do things "right"
Be fair and consistent

44

Slide 8–45

Listen for Understanding

LEVEL 1
- What's in it for me? Rebuttal, self–interest, filtering.

LEVEL 2
- Where is the person coming from? What are they truly trying to say? Connect, silence self–talk.

LEVEL 3
- What is not being said that is important? Listen through the words.

45

Slide 8–46

Reflective Listening

- Provide eye contact
- Maintain an interested and open body posture
- Encourage the speaker with verbal and nonverbal support
- Use "door opening" questions to build trust
- Ask genuine questions
- Reflect back what they've said with empathy

46

Slide 8–47

Employee Development/Coaching

- Definitions of Employee Development / Coaching
- Coaching
- Giving Effective Feedback
- Journaling

"Every blade of grass has an Angel that bends over it and whispers 'grow, grow.'"
– The Talmud

47

Slide 8–48

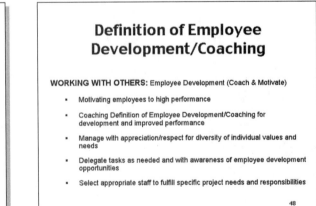

Definition of Employee Development/Coaching

WORKING WITH OTHERS: Employee Development (Coach & Motivate)

- Motivating employees to high performance
- Coaching Definition of Employee Development/Coaching for development and improved performance
- Manage with appreciation/respect for diversity of individual values and needs
- Delegate tasks as needed and with awareness of employee development opportunities
- Select appropriate staff to fulfill specific project needs and responsibilities

48

Slide 8–49

Coaching

What is reality 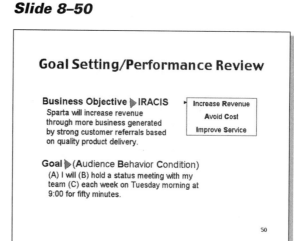 **What is desired**

What is reality	**What is desired**
Facts, no interpretation	Aligned with business, DISC, PIAV
Observable behaviors	Measurable and achievable
Employee's feelings	Desirable by all

Focus on growing talents, not fixing weaknesses.

49

Slide 8–50

Goal Setting/Performance Review

Business Objective ▶ **IRACIS**
Sparta will increase revenue
through more business generated
by strong customer referrals based
on quality product delivery.

| Increase Revenue |
| Avoid Cost |
| Improve Service |

Goal ▶ (Audience Behavior Condition)
(A) I will (B) hold a status meeting with my
team (C) each week on Tuesday morning at
9:00 for fifty minutes.

50

Slide 8–51

Coaching (continued)
BUSINESS COACHING:
Focus on business change, not personal growth.
"Therapy looks back, coaching looks forward."

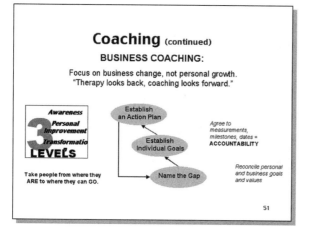

3 LEVELS
Awareness
Personal Improvement
Transformation

Take people from where they ARE to where they can GO.

Establish an Action Plan
Establish Individual Goals
Name the Gap

Agree to measurements, milestones, dates = ACCOUNTABILITY

Reconcile personal and business goals and values

51

Slide 8–52

Coaching (continued)

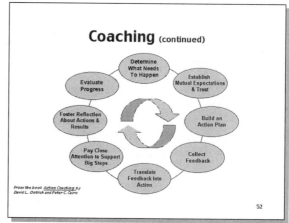

Determine What Needs To Happen
Establish Mutual Expectations & Trust
Build an Action Plan
Collect Feedback
Translate Feedback Into Action
Pay Close Attention to Support Big Steps
Foster Reflection About Actions & Results
Evaluate Progress

From the book *Action Coaching* by David L. Dotlich and Peter C. Cairo

52

Slide 8–53

Coaching Language

Avoid directing the discussion.
NOT *"No, that's the wrong goal."*

Avoid analysis and interpretation.
NOT *"Yes, I know which part bothers you the most!"*

Phrase future in the present state.
NOT *"What will your relationship be like?"*

Push to the end result, not just next step.
NOT *"Promotion is what you want."*

53

Slide 8–54

Coaching Language

Questions to help people learn and explore:

- What would happen if you asked for help in this area in which you're not so skilled?
- What's stopping you from requesting a change?
- If you died today, what regrets would you have?
- How might you deal with the conflict without resorting to a win/lose posture?
- Why do you want to lead, and why should people follow you?
- What legacy do you want to leave behind? What do you want people to say about you after you've left your current role?
- What are your vulnerabilities, and where could things fall apart?
- What can you do to renew yourself? Your team? This company?

54

Slide 8–55

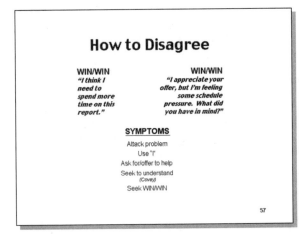

Performance Review

	No	Yes
‹ Did you discuss each goal or objective established for this employee?	▢	▢
‹ Are you and the employee clear on the areas of agreement/disagreement?	▢	▢
‹ Did you and the employee cover all positive skills, traits, accomplishments, areas of growth, etc.? Did you reinforce the employee's accomplishments?	▢	▢
‹ Did you give the employee a sense of what you thought of his or her potential or ability?	▢	▢
‹ Are you both clear on areas where improvement is required? Expected? Demanded? Desired?	▢	▢
‹ What training or development recommendations did you agree on?	▢	▢
‹ Did you indicate consequences for noncompliance, if appropriate?	▢	▢
‹ Did you set good objectives for the next appraisal period?	▢	▢
‹ Objective?	▢	▢
‹ Specific?	▢	▢
‹ Measurable?	▢	▢
‹ Standard to be used for evaluation?	▢	▢
‹ Timeframe?	▢	▢
‹ Did you set a time for the next evaluation?	▢	▢
‹ Did you confirm what your part would be? Did the employee confirm his or her part?	▢	▢
‹ Did you thank the employee for his or her efforts?	▢	▢

Provided courtesy of HRnext.com

55

Slide 8–56

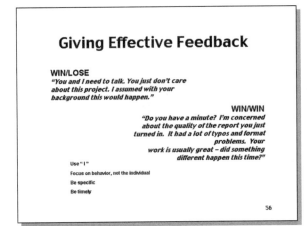

Giving Effective Feedback

WIN/LOSE
"You and I need to talk. You just don't care about this project. I assumed with your background this would happen."

WIN/WIN
"Do you have a minute? I'm concerned about the quality of the report you just turned in. It had a lot of typos and format problems. Your work is usually great – did something different happen this time?"

Use " I "

Focus on behavior, not the individual

Be specific

Be timely

56

Slide 8–57

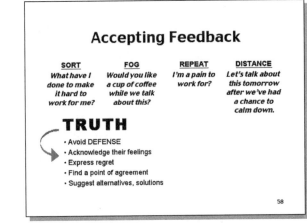

How to Disagree

WIN/WIN
"I think I need to spend more time on this report."

WIN/WIN
"I appreciate your offer, but I'm feeling some schedule pressure. What did you have in mind?"

SYMPTOMS
Attack problem
Use "I"
Ask for/offer to help
Seek to understand
(Covey)
Seek WIN/WIN

57

Slide 8–58

Accepting Feedback

SORT
What have I done to make it hard to work for me?

FOG
Would you like a cup of coffee while we talk about this?

REPEAT
I'm a pain to work for?

DISTANCE
Let's talk about this tomorrow after we've had a chance to calm down.

TRUTH
- Avoid DEFENSE
- Acknowledge their feelings
- Express regret
- Find a point of agreement
- Suggest alternatives, solutions

58

Slide 8–59

Feedback: Pointers

GIVING
Be specific, descriptive, action–oriented, nonjudgmental

RECEIVING
Be open, take notes, ask for examples, seek to understand, triangulate information later

59

Slide 8–60

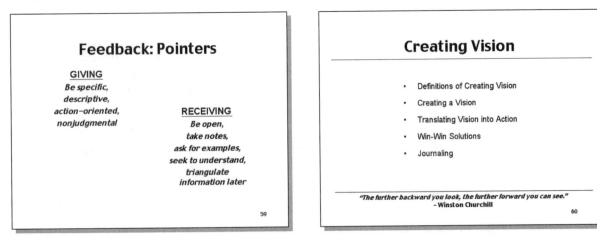

Creating Vision

- Definitions of Creating Vision
- Creating a Vision
- Translating Vision into Action
- Win-Win Solutions
- Journaling

"The further backward you look, the further forward you can see."
– Winston Churchill

60

Slide 8–61

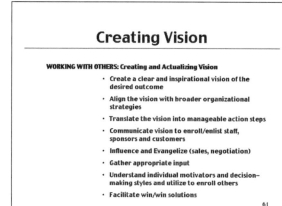

Creating Vision

WORKING WITH OTHERS: Creating and Actualizing Vision

- Create a clear and inspirational vision of the desired outcome
- Align the vision with broader organizational strategies
- Translate the vision into manageable action steps
- Communicate vision to enroll/enlist staff, sponsors and customers
- Influence and Evangelize (sales, negotiation)
- Gather appropriate input
- Understand individual motivators and decision-making styles and utilize to enroll others
- Facilitate win/win solutions

61

Slide 8–62

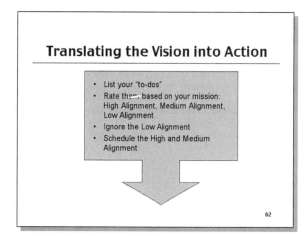

Translating the Vision into Action

- List your "to-dos"
- Rate them based on your mission: High Alignment, Medium Alignment, Low Alignment
- Ignore the Low Alignment
- Schedule the High and Medium Alignment

62

Slide 8–63

Goal Setting/Performance Review

Business Objective ▶ IRACIS

Sparta will increase revenue through more business generated by strong customer referrals based on quality product delivery.

| Increase Revenue |
| Avoid Cost |
| Improve Service |

Goal ▶ (Audience Behavior Condition)

(A) I will (B) hold a status meeting with my team (C) each week on Tuesday morning at 9:00 for 50 minutes.

63

Slide 8–64

Managing Change

- Definitions of Change
- An Overview of Change
- Change versus Transition
- Exploring the Human Side of Change
- Journaling

"Great sailors are not made of calm seas. " – Unknown

64

Slide 8–65

Exploring Change

Think about a big change that you have experienced in your life.

- What event or choice brought about the change?
- Think about the change as a process: did it happen all at once or did it unfold over time? What were some of the stages of this process?
- What were some of the challenges and successes you recall about this period of change in your life?

65

Slide 8–66

Change Versus Transition

CHANGE
- *Disruption in expectations*
- *External event*
- *Related to circumstances and situations*
- *Sometimes connected to a decision of choice*

TRANSITION
- *Psychological reorientation to the change event*
- *Internal process*
- *Related to a state of mind, a sense of identity*

66

Slide 8–67

Quotable

"It is not so much that we are afraid of change or so in love with the old ways, but it's that place in between that we fear. . . . It's like being caught between trapezes. It's Linus when his blanket is in the dryer. There's nothing to hold on to."

– Marilyn Ferguson

67

Slide 8–68

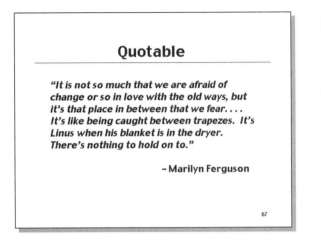

Transition: The Human Side of Change

STAGES OF TRANSITION

Source: William Bridges

68

Slide 8–69

Transition: The Human Side of Change

STAGES OF TRANSITION (continued)

Ending - Process of letting go of the old way before beginning the new form.

Neutral Zone - Fallow period between the ending and new beginning. The wilderness.

New Beginning - New status quo takes shape.

69

Slide 8–70

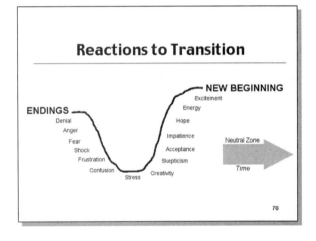

Reactions to Transition

70

Slide 8–71

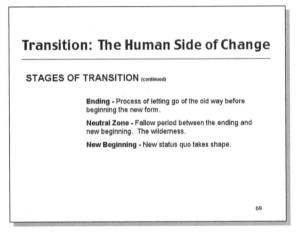

The Hero's Journey

71

Slide 8–72

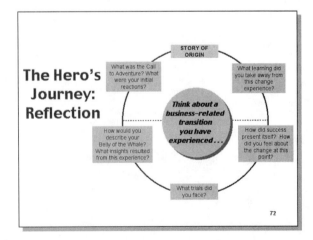

The Hero's Journey: Reflection

72

Slide 8-73

Customer Orientation

- Definitions of Customer Orientation
- Who is the Customer?
- A Consulting Focus
- Gathering requirements
- Journaling

"Be everywhere, do everything, and never fail to astonish the customer." –
Macy's Motto

73

Slide 8-74

Customer Orientation

ALIGNMENT: Customer Orientation

- Understand and apply customer needs and expectations.
- Gather customer requirements and input.
- Partner with customer in gathering requirements, maintaining communication flow and managing work.
- Set and monitor performance standards.

74

Slide 8-75

Customer Chain of Experience

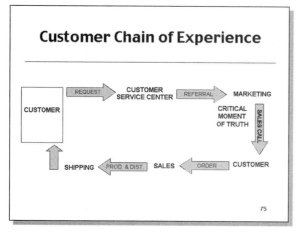

75

Slide 8-76

Shared Value

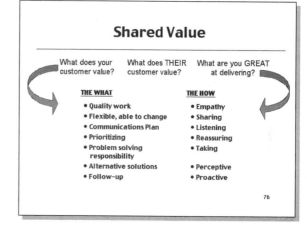

What does your customer value?	What does THEIR customer value?	What are you GREAT at delivering?

THE WHAT
- Quality work
- Flexible, able to change
- Communications Plan
- Prioritizing
- Problem solving responsibility
- Alternative solutions
- Follow-up

THE HOW
- Empathy
- Sharing
- Listening
- Reassuring
- Taking

- Perceptive
- Proactive

76

Slide 8-77

A Consulting Focus

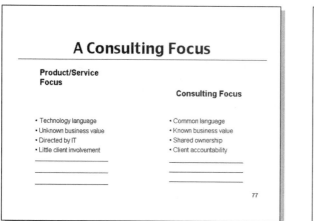

Product/Service Focus	Consulting Focus
• Technology language	• Common language
• Unknown business value	• Known business value
• Directed by IT	• Shared ownership
• Little client involvement	• Client accountability

77

Slide 8-78

Forbidden Phrases

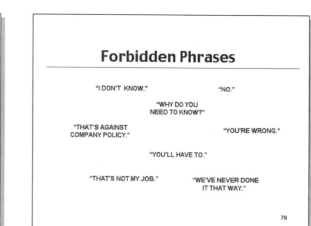

"I DON'T KNOW."   "NO."

"WHY DO YOU
NEED TO KNOW?"

"THAT'S AGAINST
COMPANY POLICY."   "YOU'RE WRONG."

"YOU'LL HAVE TO."

"THAT'S NOT MY JOB."   "WE'VE NEVER DONE
IT THAT WAY."

78

Slide 8–79

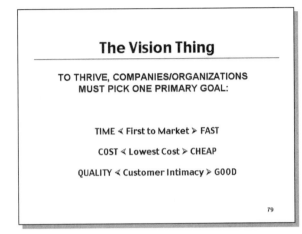

The Vision Thing

TO THRIVE, COMPANIES/ORGANIZATIONS
MUST PICK ONE PRIMARY GOAL:

TIME ≺ First to Market ≻ FAST

COST ≺ Lowest Cost ≻ CHEAP

QUALITY ≺ Customer Intimacy ≻ GOOD

79

Slide 8–80

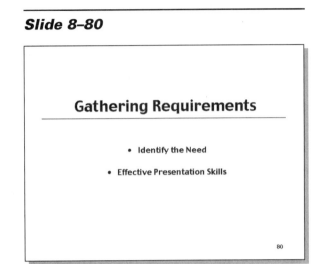

Gathering Requirements

- Identify the Need
- Effective Presentation Skills

80

Slide 8–81

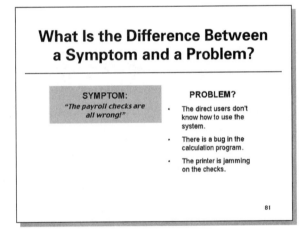

What Is the Difference Between a Symptom and a Problem?

SYMPTOM:	PROBLEM?
"The payroll checks are all wrong!"	• The direct users don't know how to use the system.
	• There is a bug in the calculation program.
	• The printer is jamming on the checks.

81

Slide 8–82

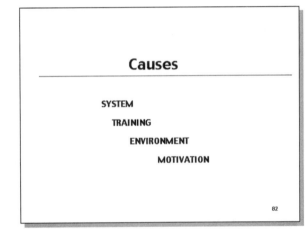

Causes

SYSTEM

TRAINING

ENVIRONMENT

MOTIVATION

82

Slide 8–83

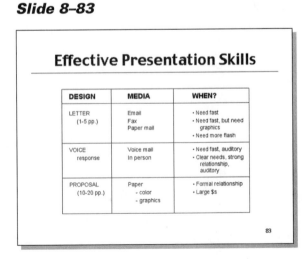

Effective Presentation Skills

DESIGN	MEDIA	WHEN?
LETTER (1-5 pp.)	Email Fax Paper mail	• Need fast • Need fast, but need graphics • Need more flash
VOICE response	Voice mail In person	• Need fast, auditory • Clear needs, strong relationship, auditory
PROPOSAL (10-20 pp.)	Paper - color - graphics	• Formal relationship • Large $s

83

Slide 8–84

What Makes People Remember?

Grass, Paper, Cat, Knife, Love, Bird, Tree,
Desk, Truth, Table, Fork, Pen, Stream,
Wisdom, Stream, Flower, Zulu, Radio,
Ruler, Blue, Sheep, Meaning, Field,
Pencil, Carbon

84

Slide 8–85

Improving Memory

PRIMACY = Remember more at the BEGINNING of a session

Remember more at the END of a session = RECENCY

Other reasons:
- Different *(ex.: Zulu)*
- Visual
- Emotion
- Organization
- Context

85

Slide 8–86

Improving Memory

- Many Breaks
- Sleep
- Attention Getter

86

Slide 8–87

WIIFM

GOOD	NOT SO GOOD
• Tells 3 – 5 people about it	• Tells 8 – 10 people about it
• Can charge more	• Costs 5 – 6 times more to attract new customers
• Can be more profitable	• Expensive
• Invaluable	• Reactive
• Proactive	

"The Rule of 10"

87

Slide 8–88

Why Do Customers Stop Being Customers?

100%

- 1% Die
- 3% Move Away
- 5% Seek alternatives
- 9% Go to the competition
- 14% Dissatisfied with product/service
- 68% Upset with the treatment they receive

Beyond Customer Service,1992.

88

Slide 8–89

Strategic Business Acumen

- Definitions of Strategic Business Acumen
- Systems Thinking
- Scenario Planning
- Group Techniques for Consensus
- Journaling

"If you can dream it, you can do it. " – Walt Disney

89

Slide 8–90

Strategic Business Acumen

ALIGNMENT:
Strategic Business Acumen

- Demonstrate ability to ethically build support for a perspective about which you feel strongly.
- Holistic view – think in terms of the entire system and the effects and consequences of actions and decisions.
- Operate with an awareness of marketplace competition and general landscape of related business arenas.
- General business acumen – functions of strategic planning, finance, marketing, manufacturing, R&D, etc.

90

Slide 8–91

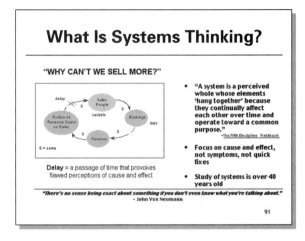

Slide 8–92

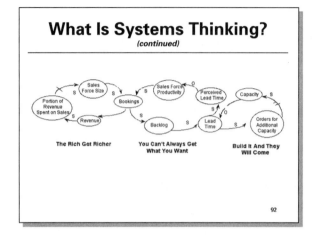

Slide 8–93

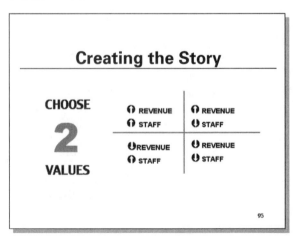

Slide 8–94

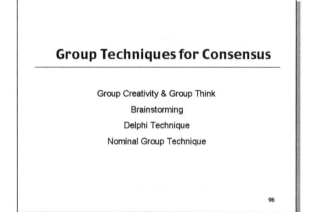

Slide 8–95

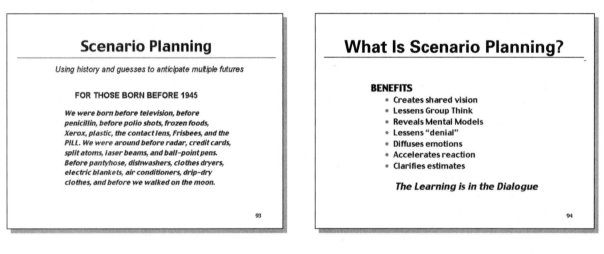

Slide 8–96

Slide 8–97

Group Creativity and Group Think

GROUP CREATIVITY
When compared to individuals,
groups make accurate decisions.

However...

GROUP THINK
An individual may feel social
pressure to conform to a popular
solution that he or she would not
have chosen individually.

"None of us is as smart as all of us." – Satchel Paige

97

Slide 8–98

Brainstorming

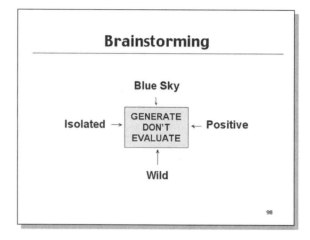

97

(Blue Sky, Isolated → GENERATE DON'T EVALUATE ← Positive, Wild)

98

Slide 8–99

Brainstorming (continued)

SET THE STAGE:

We will be spending _____ minutes brainstorming ideas about
our new system. There will be absolutely no interruptions during
this session. The purpose of this meeting is to discuss things
that the system can do for us, with the emphasis on quantity
not quality. Therefore, please be prepared to suggest several
ideas and to refrain from offering any criticism of the ideas of
others. Advance preparation is unnecessary. If you have any
questions, please contact me.

• Moderator: first ideas, one crazy
• Record ideas visually

99

Slide 8–100

The Delphi Technique

- Keep membership anonymous
- Keep specific communications anonymous
- Allow only written communications

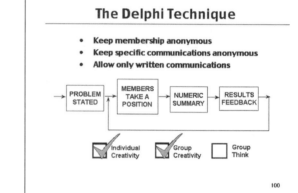

(PROBLEM STATED → MEMBERS TAKE A POSITION → NUMERIC SUMMARY → RESULTS FEEDBACK; ✓ Individual Creativity, ✓ Group Creativity, ☐ Group Think)

100

Slide 8–101

The Nominal Group Technique

- Membership is NOT anonymous
- Participation controlled by procedures
- Everyone must participate verbally

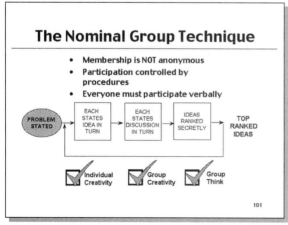

(PROBLEM STATED → EACH STATES IDEA IN TURN → EACH STATES DISCUSSION IN TURN → IDEAS RANKED SECRETLY → TOP RANKED IDEAS; ✓ Individual Creativity, ✓ Group Creativity, ✓ Group Think)

101

Slide 8–102

Project Leadership

- Definitions of Project Leadership
- What is Project Leadership?
- DEFINE the Project
- PLAN the Project
- MANAGE the Project
- REVIEW the Project
- Journaling

"Now that we're organized, what do we do?" – Unknown

102

Slide 8–103

Project Leadership

ALIGNMENT: Project Leadership

- Set, communicate and monitor milestones and objectives
- Gain and maintain buy in from sponsors and customers
- Prioritize and allocate resources
- Manage multiple, potentially conflicting priorities across various/diverse disciplines
- Maintain an effective, interactive and productive team culture
- Manage budget and project progress
- Manage risk versus reward and ROI equations
- Balance established standards with need for exceptions in decision-making
- Make timely decisions in alignment with customer and business pace

103

Slide 8–104

What Is Project Leadership?

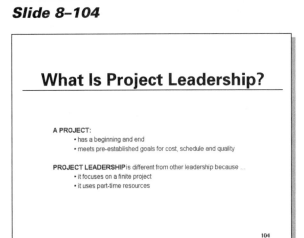

A PROJECT:
- has a beginning and end
- meets pre-established goals for cost, schedule and quality

PROJECT LEADERSHIP is different from other leadership because ...
- it focuses on a finite project
- it uses part-time resources

104

Slide 8–105

What Is Project Leadership?
(continued)

PROJECT LEADER
Plans, Organizes and Controls the Project

PROJECT TEAM MEMBERS
Perform project activities and produce project deliverables

105

Slide 8–106

Steps to Great Projects

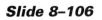

START → DEFINE → PLAN → MANAGE → REVIEW → END

DEFINE	PLAN	MANAGE	REVIEW
1. Establish project scope	1. Finalize objectives	1. Control work in progress	1. Turn over deliverables
2. Set initial objectives	2. Create schedule	2. Provide feedback	2. Hold Project Review
3. List risks/ constraints	3. Assign resources	3. Negotiate for resources	3. Release resources
4. Evaluate alternatives	4. Create budget	4. Resolve differences	4. Document successes and failures
5. Choose a course of action			

Dare to Properly Manage Resources!

106

Slide 8–107

DEFINE:
Write the Project Definition

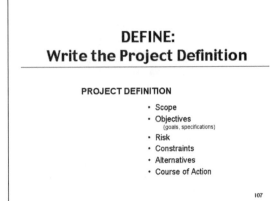

PROJECT DEFINITION

- Scope
- Objectives
  (goals, specifications)
- Risk
- Constraints
- Alternatives
- Course of Action

107

Slide 8–108

Establish Project Scope

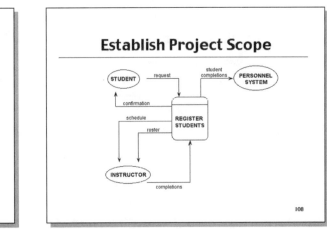

108

Slide 8–109

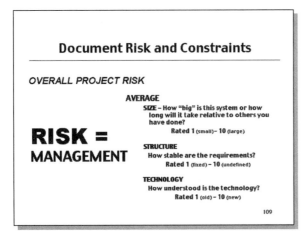

Slide 8–110

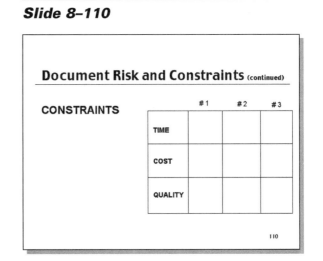

Slide 8–111

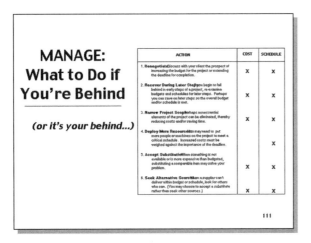

Slide 8–112

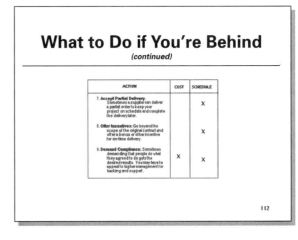

Slide 8–113

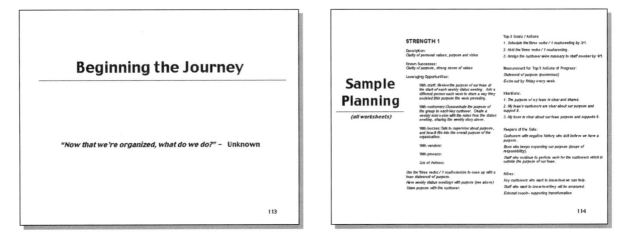

Slide 8–114

Slide 8–115

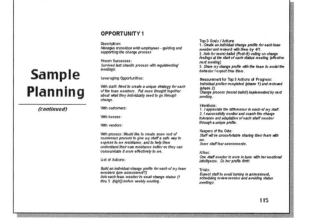

Follow-Up Work: Action Planning

What's in This Chapter?

- ◆ Teaching notes for implementing the Action Planning portion of the two-day workshop

- ◆ Options for setting up manager reviews

- ◆ Tips for coaching and follow-up sessions

- ◆ Ideas for continuing the learning about leadership

Your leadership workshop will be just the beginning of each learner's journey to growing his or her own leadership capacity. Most of the learners took more than 30 years to develop the leadership strengths and weaknesses they currently have, so it is not likely that they will be "fixed," even by a workshop as long as two days. Consider the learning event itself as part of the complete solution. The complete solution contains

- ◆ an expert learning facilitator with great content (chapters 1 and 2, 5 through 8)

- ◆ effective roles, logistics, and planning (chapter 1)

- ◆ advance work and assessment (chapter 4)

- ◆ evaluation (chapter 4)

- ◆ follow-up action planning (this chapter).

Apply this model regardless of the length of the workshop. Even a one-hour presentation benefits from a few minutes of self-assessment at the start, followed by "homework." Of course, the facilitator cannot control whether the homework gets done, and this is true regardless of the length of the event. Because of this, management support is critical to complete a leadership initiative. Chapter 1 contains more information about choosing the right solution for a client.

When you are choosing which depth of leadership event to offer to a group of learners, fight for the involvement of their management team. Creating an Action Plan will not help much if there is no incentive to complete it. Your learners must be clear that their leadership development is not only important to them, but also to their management. This chapter will explore how management can be involved in each of the following:

- setting up manager reviews
- coaching sessions
- follow-up sessions
- ideas to continue learning.

Setting Up Manager Reviews

One of the most effective ways to ensure that an Action Plan is taken seriously is to get the supervisor of the learner involved in some way. Here are a couple of options:

- Ask a high-level manager to kick off each session, stressing the importance of the Action Plan.

- Invite different leadership team members throughout the session to share their stories about some of the key competencies and why they are critical to the success of the organization.

- Send a copy of the Action Plans (with the knowledge and permission of each learner) to the supervisors for review.

- Ask the learners to set up a meeting with their supervisors to go over their Action Plans as homework.

- Ask the supervisors to come to the workshop for an hour or so and go over the Action Plans with each learner at the end of the event or over lunch.

- Two things must be done for any of these to work effectively:

  - The supervisors or leaders must have attended the training already so they are well aware of the leadership competencies, have examined their own strengths and gaps, and empathize with the learner.

◆ The supervisors or leaders must be willing to take criticism from the learners as they begin to demand better leadership and continue to grow their own.

Manager reviews can be approached in a 360-degree way. As homework, ask each learner to meet with each of his or her team members to informally listen to each worker's career goals. Review the results in a follow-up session or encourage them to review the results with their own manager. This can be the start of a stronger mentoring relationship between learner and manager as well as a stronger leadership role between learner and team members.

Coaching Sessions

Offering coaching sessions, either in person or over the phone, can help learners manage their transition into a leadership role. Many people will not feel the need to talk with a coach, but people who are very serious about improving or are frustrated with their inability to make the transition into leadership in the past may find it very useful to work with a professional coach for an hour three or four times a month until they feel more confident.

A coach's role is to be a mirror—to listen and ask questions—which helps the person being coached see more clearly their own beliefs, obstacles, and desires. Paradoxically, coaching is one of the roles in the Employee Development competency in this leadership program. I have found it very effective to learn coaching by being coached.

The coach should be completely neutral—the supervisor is probably not the right person to play this role during leadership development because he or she is also responsible for reviewing the learner. Outside coaches tend to work best because it is easier to open up to them. Many of our coaching clients work with our coaches over the phone and have never met them. The most critical aspect is that the coach be a listener and asker, but not a teller. People you work with everyday have trouble playing that role.

Follow-Up Sessions

After your leadership training sessions, you may find it useful to bring people together at three- or six-month intervals. This is a very personal journey, and people like to reconnect and support the others who have been going through the same thing.

The first follow-up should be done within six months at the most. There is a stronger reinforcement of the learning if you can schedule a brief follow-up within three months.

For the session, create an agenda with the following:

- work to be brought to class (see previous sections) for discussion
- challenges to discuss
- resources that have been helpful.

You may have a situation in which the company is willing to invest in significant follow-up. When this is the case, follow up with a half- or full-day every other month or so on one competency. Step through each of the 10 competencies with the same team. This goes a long way in changing the culture of leadership.

In addition, try to get leaders into the follow-up sessions as well. Recruit them as guest experts or invite them for a lunch or coffee break. Work hard to integrate the leadership that exists with the leadership to come.

Ideas for Continuing Learning

Be prepared to offer your learners multiple resources to help them continue learning. Many of these can be found in the Resources section of this book. Here are some other ideas that you might investigate:

- listservs or electronic newsletters with a leadership slant (or start your own for alumni)
- articles and magazines pertaining to leadership
- books
- self-paced e-learning or Websites with leadership-oriented topics
- videos or DVDs with stories of successful leaders (not just corporate leaders)
- leadership and coaching professional development groups.

Summary

Growing leadership is a journey, not an event. Follow-up work, with multiple offerings, provides a way to help the learner return and review his or her Action Plan. Management involvement, though difficult to get at first, is critical to making a real corporate culture change.

What to Do Next

- ◆ Design the Action Plan strategy that makes the most sense for your solution.

- ◆ Implement the strategy.

Learning Activities

- Detailed instructions for using the 23 learning activities
- Tips for trainers

This chapter presents all of the learning activities included in the training agendas in chapters 5 through 8. The slides referred to in each of the learning activities in this chapter are numbered according to the order in which they appear in each PowerPoint presentation (one-hour, half-day, one-day, and two-day). You can choose individual slides to suit your customized content by opening the file you want to change, saving the file under a different name, and deleting slides you do not want to use. Use the thumbnails of the slides to copy from one length of presentation to another.

Tips for Trainers

Before using these learning activities in your training sessions, be sure to review chapters 1 through 4 for background on how this training program was developed and how it can be used. Chapter 2 includes tips on facilitation, including preparation, room setup and customizing the program to different audiences.

As in all training, adding your personal touch by sharing your own stories will help make the content come alive. Feel free to describe your experiences with good and bad leadership whenever those examples might be helpful. Customizing the learning activities with examples from your organization also will add value to the program.

Be flexible. The timeframes for many of these activities can be changed according to your own goals and needs. You may find that you cover key concepts in the course of discussion and that you no longer need to include certain activities or content.

Learning Activity 10–1:
Understanding Leadership

GOALS

The goals of this activity are to

- ◆ introduce the concept of leadership

- ◆ begin to identify each participant's leadership strengths and weaknesses

- ◆ be aware of the 10 leadership competencies.

MATERIALS

- ◆ flipchart and marking pen

TIME

- ◆ 20 minutes

INSTRUCTIONS

Ask the people in the room to divide into groups of three to five members and choose their group leaders. Explain to them that the leaders will be the person in each group with the most children—obviously a person with a great deal of leadership experience. If a group has a tie, ask it to use the greatest number of pets as a tiebreaker.

Now explain that each team will have three minutes to strategize before the project begins. Then flip to the following project instructions that you have printed on a flipchart (if you prefer, you could add a page with these instructions to your PowerPoint file, but I prefer that the learners *not* have a copy so it is more of a surprise): "The goal of your project is to build the tallest structure possible with the coins currently in the possession of your team. You will have five minutes to complete the project."

Explain that they will have five minutes to implement the project after strategizing. Immediately instruct the team to begin strategizing. Act as if there is no need for further instruction. If a team comes to you with questions, answer them individually.

After three minutes, tell the teams to begin implementing their projects. Watch and listen to the leadership strategies and notice who is playing the role of leader. Many teams may be done before five minutes have passed, but having a little more time will get them to think a bit more broadly and challenge their original strategies. This is a tremendous test of flexible leadership, so watch this occur. If people come in late, ask them to help you observe.

Be mindful because this exercise can cause people to do some crazy things—stand on tables, climb walls, and so on. Let it go as long as it makes sense and doesn't threaten anyone's safety.

At completion of the five minutes, ask each team to show its project results. Avoid deciding who is the winner and congratulate everyone. Go to the flipchart and ask the teams to answer the following questions (one on each side of the same page):

- ◆ What leadership qualities helped your project succeed?

- ◆ What lack of leadership qualities challenged your project?

Encourage people not just to think about the qualities of the "formal" leaders (assigned by your criteria) but also of the informal leaders. Capture all the results of this discussion on the flipchart and use these to reinforce the 10 competencies, especially Self-Awareness (which is the primary focus of this module). To complete the discussion, ask each team, on the count of three, to point to the person on the team who was the primary task leader. Then have them point to the person who was the primary people leader. Encourage people to think of all the different components of leadership and remind them that they don't all end up in the same person.

Learning Activity 10–2: Lead/Manage

GOALS

The goals of this activity are to

* think about the difference between managing and leading

* build rapport and trust among participants.

MATERIALS

* PowerPoint Slides 8–7 through 8–10

* Handout 11–1: The 10 Leadership Competencies

* blank paper and pen/pencil for each participant

TIME

* 20 minutes

INSTRUCTIONS

Ask people to work with the others at their table (preferably three to five participants). The leader of each team will be the person with the most children, and the tiebreaker will be the greatest number of pets. Explain that you will give each team an opportunity to brainstorm and write down as many word associations as possible for *Lead* and *Manage*. When you say "go," they will have one minute to brainstorm as many words as possible that describe *Lead*. When you say to switch, they will have another minute to brainstorm as many words as possible that describe *Manage*. Here's an example:

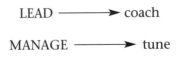

LEAD ──────→ coach

MANAGE ──────→ tune

After the brainstorming is over, ask for two volunteers—a right-handed person and a left-handed person. Put the left-handed person on the right side of the flipchart and the right-handed volunteer on the left side. Explain that you are going to gather the results of the brainstorming by asking each group to quickly share one word association for each term. The left-handed volunteer will log the *Lead* words, the right-handed person will log the *Manage* words. With your help, they should be able to move this through very quickly. Go for about three rounds of positive and negative words for the two words with all the teams.

Use these words to explain the difference between *Manage* ("work hard") and *Lead* ("work smart"). Show PowerPoint slide 8–7 and leave it up while teams work. Read through slides 8–8 and 8–9. Use slide 8–10 to introduce the three categories of leadership competencies covered in this workshop: Self-Alignment, Working with Others, and Integration. Use Handout 11–1: The 10 Leadership Competencies (chapter 11, page 148) so that people have a reference as the workshop progresses. Explain that growing leadership requires that we explore our Self, learn to work well with others, but most importantly learn to integrate the right tools and techniques, with the right people, for the right task, at the right time.

Learning Activity 10–3: Personal Mission

GOAL

The goal of this activity is to help participants identify their own personal missions.

MATERIALS

- flipchart and marking pen

- tentcards and pen/pencil for each pair of participants

TIME

- 20 minutes

INSTRUCTIONS

To help people get started, lead a quick brainstorming session asking each person to share a verb while you write these on the flipchart. Start the list with such words as

◆ ignite	◆ enable
◆ affirm	◆ monitor
◆ sustain	◆ grow
◆ support	

Then brainstorm nouns:

◆ technology	◆ people
◆ customers	◆ learning
◆ products	◆ knowledge

Ask the learners to create a personal mission statement using three verbs and one noun. Explain that they can add words to make the statement more meaningful; for example, "Create, Teach, and Encourage Compliance Standards" makes more sense if it's written "Create, Teach, and Encourage Compliance to Company Standards." It is best to make these as specific as you can, so adding adjectives and adverbs is fine. Give people 10 minutes or so (watch to see when people are done). Play some quiet instrumental music while people work on this.

Give each learner a tent card. Ask each of them to partner with another learner and share their personal mission statements. Have the pairs work together to refine and clarify their personal missions. When they are content with what they have, ask them to write their mission statement boldly (in marker) on the front of the tent card.

Learning Activity 10–4: Self-Assessment

GOAL

The goal of this activity is to begin to assess the learners' individual leadership strengths and weaknesses.

MATERIALS

- ◆ Assessment 11–1: Leadership Self-Assessment
- ◆ flipchart and marking pen

TIME

- ◆ 20 minutes

INSTRUCTIONS

Explain the groupings of Self-Alignment, Working with Others, and Integration, and note the competencies contained in each. Point out that growing as leaders requires that we explore our inner Self and learn to work well with others, and most importantly learn to integrate the right tools and techniques, with the right people, for the right task, at the right time. This is the magic of leadership.

Distribute Assessment 11–1: Leadership Self-Assessment (chapter 11, page 169). Ask learners to look at each of the subcompetencies, evaluate their own competency by writing H (high), M (medium), or L (low), then summarize all the subcompetencies and come up with an overall rating of H, M, or L for each competency. Do the first one as an example so they understand the process. Play quiet instrumental music while participants work on their own.

Learning Activity 10–5: Behavioral Style

GOAL

The goal of this activity is to begin to assess the learners' individual behavioral styles.

MATERIALS

- Assessment 11–2: Quick n' Dirty DISC/PIAV

- PowerPoint slides 8–13 through 8–17 (depending on length of program)

- flipchart and marking pen

TIME

- 20 minutes

INSTRUCTIONS

Distribute Assessment 11–2: Quick n' Dirty DISC/PIAV (chapter 11, page 172). Have participants circle all the words on both pages that they feel apply to them. If you are holding the two-day program, show PowerPoint slide 8–13 while they do this. Explain that a higher number of words circled in a quadrant suggests that they exhibit more of this type of behavior, but note that this is not scientific. Ask people to notice the quadrant with the most circles, as well as any quadrants with none.

Explain that sometimes a good way to jumpstart understanding oneself is through assessments. DISC (Dominance, Influence, Steadiness, and Compliance) assessments measure how a person behaves and how others would describe his or her behavior. PIAV (Personal Interests, Attitudes, and Values) assessments measure how a person prioritizes, to what he or she is drawn, and what he or she avoids. This assessment is a nonscientific shortcut to get people thinking about their own difference. It is highly recommended, especially in the longer version of the workshop, that you license and use the full DISC and PIAV profiles from a distributor in order to get adequate depth of understanding. There are many different companies that distribute DISC assessments and several that distribute PIAV assessments (see the Resources section for more information).

Explaining the Self-Assessments

Using PowerPoint slide 8–13 (5–7, 6–6, or 7–6, depending on the program length) begin to explain the D, I, S, and C behaviors, using the explanation below. The shading on this slide indicates how it might look for a person who has had his or her full profile done. The next slide is a different chart based on the same assessment. For additional reading on these behaviors, please look in the Resources section. I highly recommend *The Four Dimensional Manager* (Straw, 2002).

- **D indicates Dominance.** Note that the words under the D and above the energy line grow in their sense of urgency. D behavior tries to complete tasks as quickly as possible. The two key words for D are Urgent and Task.

- **I indicates Influence.** Note that the words close above the energy line for I indicate more focus on influencing people through people skills, whereas the words below the line influence through facts. I behavior will try to influence people as quickly as possible. The two key words for I are Urgent and People.

- **S indicates Steadiness.** Note that the words above the line for S indicate a focus on people, but with much more care and diligence than an I. S likes things to stay steady and for everyone to be happy. The two key words for S are Diligent and People.

- **C indicates Compliance.** Note that the words above the energy line for C indicate a focus on detailed tasks, moving toward perfection. C likes to complete tasks perfectly and doesn't like to be rushed. The two key words for C are Diligent and Task.

Emphasize that the farther above the middle line shown in the slide, the more active the behavior, and the farther below the line the more passive the behavior. The learners' quadrants could have one or a few circles that are close to the line. These behaviors are called situational; they may be adopted depending on circumstances, but are not necessarily preferences.

If you are conducting the two-day program, show slide 8–15, Adapted Style. For other lengths, show slide 5–8, 6–6, or 7–6, depending on the program length. Some DISC profiles allow you to assess your "happy place," which is shown on this slide as the Natural profile, and how you are adapting your behaviors to deal with your current situation, which is shown as the Adapted profile. The more adapting, especially over that midway line, the more stress in a person's life. Using this slide, explain that everyone must adapt situationally to get along well with others but that the more people adapt by crossing above or below the main energy line on a regular basis—for example, to fit into a job that is not the best job for their natural style—the more stress they receive. Adaptation is better as temporary change than as a lifestyle.

Show the PowerPoint slide 8–16 (5–9, 6–7, or 7–7, depending on the program length). For additional reading on these behaviors, please look in the Resources section of this book. This slide shows the values assessed by the second page of the Quick n' Dirty DISC/PIAV assessment or the PIAV report participants received if they completed the full assessment. This profile is not distributed by as wide a group of companies as the DISC. With the full assessment, the learners should turn to this page in their own reports, which should be approximately two pages from the end. Ask the participants to look at the Top Two and Bottom Two values and the words they circled there. The Top Two values are where people spend as much of their energy as they can. The Bottom Two are values that they not only do not value or understand, but also may even find distasteful in others. It's easy to see how some people might not get along based on these. Here are the values explained:

- **Theoretical:** A person with this value seeks learning new things and new experiences.

- **Utilitarian:** A person with this value seeks return-on-investment in all ways, but often focused on money.

- **Aesthetic:** A person with this value seeks beauty, harmony, and balance.

- **Social:** A person with this value is concerned with everyone else and wants to save all the people in the world.

- **Individualist:** A person with this value seeks power and prestige.

- **Traditional:** A person with this value follows exactly and attempts to convert others to their tradition, which could be religion, politics, or other "rules to live by."

Show PowerPoint slide 8–17 (5–10, 6–8, or 7–8, depending on the program length), which shows the values another way. It is easy to see the top two and bottom two with this view. The situational values would be the middle two (Tra and Soc)—the person may choose these values when the situation warrants it, but they are not a passion. The small dark line indicates the average of all U.S. profiles done and shows how likely you are to run into a person who prefers a value more or less than you.

The point of showing the participants these slides is to help them see how different people are and how diverse leadership must be to meet the needs of all people. It also helps people understand the source of conflict.

An option would be to replace these four slides with slides for the assessments with which you are most comfortable (for example, Myers-Briggs or Herrmann Brain Dominance Instrument).

Learning Activity 10–6: Resiliency Attitude

GOALS

The goals of this activity are to

- introduce the competency of resilience

- begin to think about how our attitude affects our resiliency.

MATERIALS

- one blank sheet of paper for each participant

TIME

- 20 minutes

INSTRUCTIONS

Explain that this is a drawing exercise. Ask each person to take the blank piece of paper and divide it into quadrants. Some will groan that they can't draw. Tell them that they're going to draw four things, one at a time, and that you'll allow 15 seconds for each drawing. Have the group prepare to draw in the quadrant on the upper right. When everyone is ready, with your eye on the clock, ask them to draw a house. Keep time. When time's up move to quadrant two, on the lower right. Ask them to draw with their other hand (righties use their left and vice versa). When they are ready, give them 15 seconds to draw a cat. When time's up tell them to switch writing implements back to the preferred hand and move to quadrant three. Tell them to draw a flower with their eyes closed. When time's up have the participants close their eyes and use their other hand to draw a tree.

When the drawings are complete, ask someone to reflect on how his or her attitude changed through this exercise—how he or she was feeling and thinking about the various drawings. Differentiate between product and process: They were focusing on the product while you were paying attention to the process. Share your observations on the process that took place as they were creating their works of art.

Typically what happens is this: After drawing the house, no one really speaks. It's quiet. Some people usually cover up their work so no one else will see it. They have an expectation about their ability to draw a house based on the fact that they've been drawing houses since they were three years old. Their performance expectation on this makes them feel perhaps a little shy or shameful that their work is not better. When they moved to the cat, though, things changed. When they are finished drawing their cats, people generally laugh. They offer feedback to one another—both ribbing feedback and complimentary feedback. Because they were handicapped by using their weakest hands, their expectations of their performance were not as high; therefore they were more free to express themselves and do the best they could without shame. So it goes, through the drawing of the cat, flower, and tree. People become more and more open and less inhibited.

So what does all of this have to do with attitude and change? Explain that the point is that our world of rapid and relentless change forces us to operate as if we were "opposite-handed and eyes closed." We are not drawing houses any longer. Doing work that we've had years to learn and perfect is no longer an option. We are all handicapped by the pace of change. In order to manage that handicap, we must adopt an attitude of doing the best we can with what we've got. Note that this is not permission to slack off totally, but rather permission to cut ourselves a little slack. It highlights the need to recognize that we are all on a perpetual learning curve and that there is no shame in learning so long as we do our best. Managing change is largely attitudinal.

Learning Activity 10–7: Intake Styles

GOALS

The goals of this activity are to

◆ identify your own communication styles

◆ learn to adapt your communication styles to others.

MATERIALS

◆ Assessment 11–3: The Language System Diagnostic Instrument (one for each participant)

TIME

◆ 30 minutes

INSTRUCTIONS

You have already read about intake (communication) styles in chapter 2, but here is an additional summary of this information. Emphasize to people that this assessment shows the diversity of ways people communicate and prefer to receive information. The danger is that we believe everyone else needs the same communication behavior as we do, and that is not the case.

Explain that studies on how individuals prefer to receive new information have been conducted for years in the field of Neuro-Linguistic Programming (NLP). These fall into the categories of Visual, Auditory, and Kinesthetic.

Each leader uses a combination of these three intake styles. Some might fall strongly into one category, some have no preference between two, and some are equally able with all three. Intake styles are not the same as intelligence: Whether you prefer to learn by seeing, hearing, or doing has no bearing on how intelligent you are; it just determines your preference for receiving or sending information.

Explain that it is easy to identify their own preference(s) and guess someone else's preference(s) from certain physical characteristics that track with these preferences. Visual learners prefer books or videos, tend to speak quickly and at a somewhat high pitch, look up when they are thinking; and use language like, "I see what you mean." Sixty to 72 percent of the population prefers to learn this way. Auditory learners prefer speeches, discussions, or tapes; speak slowly and quietly; look straight ahead when they are thinking; and use language like, "I can hear what you are saying." They make up 12 to 18 percent of the population. Finally, kinesthetic learners prefer to try something, speak quickly and with great changes in intonation and body language; look down when thinking; and use language like "I get it."

Although across the general population 18 to 30 percent prefer to learn kinesthetically, I have found that there is a higher percentage of both kinesthetic and auditory preferences in technical occupations than these averages suggest. Also, note that training people (like you) tend to be kinesthetic.

Ask for a show of hands see how many learners have each of the three styles as their number-one preference. Explain that the preference percentages tend to fluctuate based on people's fields of work. Explain that when someone is trying to communicate something new to someone (as a leader would often do), he or she tends to communicate in the way he or she prefers to receive communication, reflecting his or her own preferences. For example, if he or she is a visual learner, he or she will tend to create beautiful graphics and fancy documents to communicate. But if the client is an auditory learner, he or she doesn't want the pictures, but words—fast and brief. This mismatch creates a barrier to communication that can often grow into conflict. Almost universally, information that people only have been told will not be retained—the percentage of people who prefer to hear information is usually low. Information that has been reinforced visually and kinesthetically, along with the telling, will be retained more effectively.

Learning Activity 10–8: Imposing Order on Chaos

GOAL

The goal of this activity is to think about action versus analysis.

MATERIALS

- ◆ PowerPoint slide 8–25

TIME

- ◆ 5 minutes

INSTRUCTIONS

Show the slide and give people time to read it. Ask them to decide the first five actions they would take. Give them several minutes for this.

Ask people to write down the first five things they would do after they read slide 8–25. No, there are no right answers—whatever the learners come up with is fine (actually, I don't even have them share their thoughts). The idea is that the participants engaged a process for setting priorities, just as they need to engage a process for setting priorities in the midst of change.

This exercise grew from some research on decision making that was conducted with emergency response teams. The research question was, How do these emergency response crew leaders make fast, life-and-death decisions in the midst of the chaos surrounding them? The trick lies in the question they ask themselves. Many of us approach chaos with the question of What do I do? Asking this puts us in the middle of the chaos—we get caught up in it and are overwhelmed by it. A better question to ask is What's going on? This puts us outside the chaos in observation mode. We're now in the helicopter at 100 feet looking for the pattern, getting a sense of the chaos, and the priority of actions becomes clearer. Organizational change is chaos, just like the chaos that exists at an accident scene. If we put ourselves in the middle of the mess, we'll be overwhelmed. We need to learn to ask the question the emergency response crew leaders ask, thus moving ourselves outside the chaos and knowing that the priorities will reveal themselves.

Learning Activity 10–9: Sabotage

GOALS

The goals of this activity are to

◆ learn how trust affects team behavior

◆ learn how trust affects business productivity.

MATERIALS

◆ Handout 11–10: The Sabotage Exercise

◆ Handout 11–11: Team Member Assignment Cards

◆ two decks of playing cards for each team of three to five people.

◆ flipchart and marking pen

TIME

◆ 30 minutes

INSTRUCTIONS

Before beginning the workshop using this exercise, print double-sided (and laminate if possible) the cards found in Handout 11–11: Team Member Assignment Cards (chapter 11, page 159). This will allow you to secretly set up the following four situations:

	Has a saboteur	Thinks the team has a saboteur
Team A	No	No
Team B	Yes	Yes
Team C	No	Yes
Team D	Yes	No

The first handout shows the number of cards you should make based on four teams with four people in each. If you have more or fewer people, you can adjust the number of cards, or have two of one of the teams above. For more than 16 people, just create more team cards for each team. For fewer than 16 people consider eliminating Team B and then, if necessary, Team D. You cannot play this successfully without at least two teams.

Hand one of the team assignment cards to each member of the A team. Then hand one to each member of the B team, and so on through all of the teams. Ask each person to read the information on the card silently.

Have everyone silently read through the instructions on Handout 11–10: The Sabotage Exercise (chapter 11, page 158) then give each team 5 minutes (or less) to strategize on how to approach this problem.

As facilitator, you will hand each team a deck of shuffled cards to sort (keep the teams to three to five people or you may have trouble managing them all). You could also ask for volunteers to do this for you to even up the number of people on the teams. Sometimes it is helpful to have people from the class be observers or card shufflers/observers.

Be aware of where the saboteurs are if you can because they may mess up their decks in subtle ways. Every time a team finishes, check their deck (quickly) and then give them a new deck of shuffled cards. Teams score by sorting decks. After five minutes, stop play and declare a winner (give prizes if you can).

Debrief using the following questions and any of your own, collecting ideas on the flipchart to keep them in mind:

- Which teams had saboteurs? (ask for a show of hands)

- Who do you think your saboteur was and why?

- Please raise your hand if you were a saboteur.

- Why were some of the folks picked as saboteurs and others weren't?

- Which team was the most productive? Why?

- Which team was the least productive? Why?

- How did different behavioral styles affect your working together?

- Did everyone participate equally? Why or why not?

- Was your first thought to seek to understand differences or did you assume someone was a saboteur?

- How does DISC/PIAV influence the ease or difficulty in this activity?

- How did trust affect the productivity of the teams? (The Big Question!)

Learning Activity 10–10: Coaching Role Play

GOALS

The goals of this activity are to

- experience conflict and coaching challenges

- improve your ability to coach others.

MATERIALS

- Handout 11–2 for Chuck role players

- Handout 11–3 for Angela role players

- Handout 11–4 for all participants

TIME

- 45 minutes

INSTRUCTIONS

Learners are often very fearful of role plays so emphasize the "team" nature of this to make sure they feel safe about participating. Take time reading through the instructions on the handout and split the group into teams of six, if possible. Teams should have a minimum of four people—you must have two to play each role. If the class doesn't divide into six evenly, add or subtract observers and assign the two roles to pairs in each group. The pairs will decide who will actually play the role. Again, emphasize that the observers should observe only, not offer advice or participate in any way (they'll have their chance later).

Ask the observers to use Handout 11–4. Chuck role players use Handout 11–2 and Angela role players use Handout 11–3. Ask participants not to read any other pages but the one that goes with their role.

This role play gives the participants a safe opportunity to practice coaching, which is often one of the weakest competencies. The scripts ensure that there is practice with conflict and there is a need to negotiate. Everyone is narrow in their view of reality, making this coaching situation very real.

The key is that two people at least are assigned to each role. The handout gives them the description of the problem and the perspective of their role only. In other words, when playing a role, a person only knows his or her own reality, which is different from the reality of another person. Two people strategize how to role-play Chuck, for example, and then together pick who will actually play the role. At any time, either member of the pair (the player or the partner/observer) can ask to freeze the action and huddle to come up with a new strategy. The facilitator can let them go (playing the parts) until there is some resolution or it has come to a standstill, usually in 10 minutes or less.

Spend a great deal of time debriefing (this is where the learning occurs). Ask everyone to read the other pages. While they are doing this, write on a flipchart "Leadership Lessons Learned." Then ask the observers to share their thoughts from the observation checklist. Add these to the flipchart and reinforce the day's material from what they've noticed. Don't be afraid to add your own observations, but let the observers go first. Then ask the role players for feedback.

Learning Activity 10–11: Blending Styles

GOALS

The goals of this activity are to

♦ learn how to adapt behavior to connect with someone whose behavior is not the same

♦ differentiate between dysfunctional and functional behavior adaptation.

MATERIALS

♦ Training Instrument 11–7: Blending of Styles

♦ a copy of the report from his or her DISC profile for each participant

♦ flipchart and marking pen

TIME

♦ 15 minutes

INSTRUCTIONS

Ask learners to guess where the most conflict occurs. Remind them of the following DISC information (you might draw a 2 × 2 grid on the flipchart as seen in Figure 10–1).

♦ **D: Dominance**—High focus on Task; high focus on Speed

♦ **I: Influence**—High focus on People; high focus on Speed

♦ **S: Steadiness**—High focus on People; low focus on Speed

♦ **C: Compliant**—High focus on Task; low focus on Speed.

Clearly, the most difficulty comes where Task and People are in opposition and where Speed is also in opposition. In other words, the most conflict can occur between a C and an I or between an S and a D. Less conflict occurs when only one dimension is different. The same profiles can create conflict; for example, two Ds with different agendas can make each other crazy, as can two Cs with different internal rules, especially because neither is focused on

Figure 10–1

Styles Grid

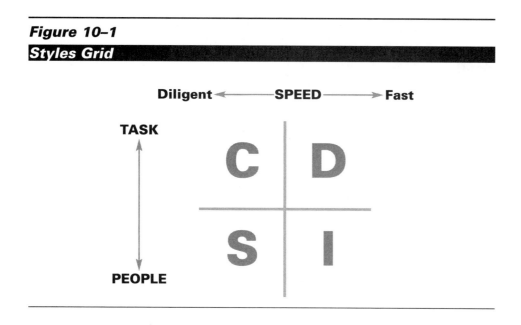

people issues. Ask learners to focus on the combinations that include their own strengths and weaknesses—with whom are they most likely to have trouble communicating?

Learning Activity 10–12: Adapting Styles

GOALS

The goals of this activity are to

- practice adapting behavior to connect with someone whose behavior is not the same

- experience the energy required to adapt and learn to invest one's energy wisely.

MATERIALS

- Training Instrument 11–8: Walk a Mile in My Shoes . . .

- a copy of the report from each learner's DISC profile

TIME

- 20 minutes

INSTRUCTIONS

For 10 minutes, each participant will work in a team of three to five and practice acting like a person with the profile that is most unlike them. Ask everyone to read the first or second scenario in Training Instrument 11–8: Walk a Mile in My Shoes (chapter 11, page 187). You will probably not have time to do both scenarios. If you can, you may want to replace these scenarios with two that are common in your learners' work environment to make this exercise more real.

Each learner will pick a behavioral style that is not his or her strength to use while the scenario is discussed, but will not tell the others. The learners will discuss the scenario using their adapted style for five minutes. If you have enough people, pull out one person at each table to act as an observer.

Debrief using the following questions:

- What was the hardest thing to do when you were adapting?

- Does adapting take more or less energy? Why? What would happen if you tried to do this for long periods of time?

Briefly ask for volunteers (or observers) to share how they adapted to each of the DISC styles.

Learning Activity 10–13: Listening

GOALS

The goals of this activity are to

- practice reflective listening

- review the experiences and lesson learned during the day.

MATERIALS

- None

TIME

- 10 minutes

INSTRUCTIONS

Quickly divide the learners into pairs. Ask each person to share his or her most important learning points for the day for two minutes. The other person, the listener, will practice reflective listening. After this two-minute period, have the participants switch roles and repeat. As a group, talk about what was hard, what worked well, and what they'd like to carry forward.

Learning Activity 10–14: Feedback

GOALS

The goals of this activity are to

- identify the learners' personal feedback styles

- improve their ability to coach others.

MATERIALS

- Handout 11–12 (for all participants)

- Handout 11–13 (for the Leader only)

- two flipcharts and two marking pens

TIME

- 30 minutes

INSTRUCTIONS

Ask everyone to break into groups of three. The Leader will be the one who is the oldest of the three. The Observer will be the one who is the youngest. All he or she does is watch what happens (and emphasize that the observer should not participate in what happens between the other two at all). The third person is the Team Member. Have all three read the directions on Handout 11–12: Feedback (chapter 11, page 161).

Explain that the Leader's job in this exercise will be to coach and help the Team Member, whose role is to solve the puzzles in the handout within five minutes. Only the Leader can look at Handout 11–13: Hints and Solutions for Feedback (chapter 11, page 162). The leaders are privy to a bit more information (just as leaders often are), but the Team Member cannot look at this. Ask for any questions and begin quickly. At this point, the Leaders will be a bit puzzled because you have given them the answers and they don't know whether they have permission to just tell the Team Member the answers. Be evasive and avoid answering that question.

Hurry into the exercise, saying, "Go!" Play "rushed" instrumental music and announce the time remaining every minute to aggravate them. Call time at five minutes.

Ask everyone to look at the solutions and share how successful they were. If appropriate, reward the winning teams.

Ask for the Observers' thoughts first, and then get opinions from the Leaders and Team Members for each question:

1. What kind of effective feedback did you see from Leader to Team Member?

2. What kind of effective feedback did you see from Team Member to Leader?

3. How did time pressures affect the feedback from Leader to Team Member?

4. How did time pressures affect the feedback from Team Member to Leader?

5. What hindered effective feedback from Leader to Team Member?

6. What hindered effective feedback from Team Member to Leader?

Write on the flipchart "Things to Remember about Feedback, Leadership, and Coaching." Use two flipcharts and volunteer scribes. Put a happy face on top of one and a sad face on top of the other. Under these write positive things that were learned during this exercise (happy-face page) and things to avoid (sad-face page).

Learning Activity 10–15: Creating a Vision

GOAL

The goal of this activity is to help participants identify their organization's or business's vision.

MATERIALS

- tent cards on which participants can write (should be able to use the back side of the ones used for Learning Activity 10–3)
- PowerPoint slides 8–60 and 8–61

TIME

- 15 minutes

INSTRUCTIONS

This is essentially the same as Learning Activity 10–3: Personal Mission, but this time the learners are creating a vision for their organizations or businesses using three verbs and a noun. Have people work individually for the first five minutes to come up with the vision. Explain that they can add words to make the statement meaningful; for example, "Create, Teach, and Encourage Compliance Standards" makes more sense if it's written "Create, Teach, and Encourage Compliance with Company Standards." It is best to make these as specific as you can, so adding adjectives and adverbs is fine. Play some quiet instrumental music while people work on this.

Guide the learners through slide 8–60 and then show and discuss slide 8–61. Build teams of three to five people who work for the same organization or business and ask them to come to consensus about their business vision. Ask each team to share and then ask each participant to write his or her business vision on the back of the name tent card on which they previously wrote their personal missions.

Learning Activity 10–16: Customer Orientation

GOAL

The goal of this activity is to help participants adopt a customer orientation.

MATERIALS

+ PowerPoint slides 8–73 through 8–76

TIME

+ 30 minutes

INSTRUCTIONS

Introduce the customer orientation competency, using slides 8–73 and 8–74. Break the class into groups of three to five people. Using slide 8–75, tell a story about a customer's call to a call center concerning a product problem (use this one or replace with one more consistent with your audience). The call is routed internally to the marketing area, which has a salesperson contact the customer to initiate an order to get the repair done. Eventually this order trickles through shipping and ends up at the customer. Notice that all the players are doing exactly what they are supposed to do, but there is very little feedback to the customer. Make the following points:

+ Everyone in this system is "sane" from his or her perspective. The system as a whole becomes "insane."

+ No one is communicating status with the customer. No one owns the issue.

+ Critical moments of truth are contacts with the customer—such as call center, salesperson, or shipped product—but there are also more subtle contacts, such as commercials, voice mail, or automated caller system.

Ask each person to take a minute and share the story of her or his worst customer ever with the team. The facilitator should keep track of time and say "Switch" when time is up. At the end, have each team select the "best" worst story to share with the whole class. Ask one team to tell its worst customer story now. When this is done, ask the person to tell the story again from the customer's perspective. Now identify the key critical moments of truth. Repeat quickly for each team if time allows. Use slide 8–76 and the questions on it to emphasize the lessons learned from these stories.

Learning Activity 10–17: STEM

GOAL

The goal of this activity is to help participants separate the symptoms of a customer problem from its cause.

MATERIALS

◆ PowerPoint slides 8–81 and 8–82

TIME

◆ 10 minutes

INSTRUCTIONS

Ask your group how the following symptom could indicate a problem in the areas of System (software or hardware), Training (skills or knowledge gap), Environment (anything in place that can cause inefficiencies, such as process, work culture, or illness), or Motivation (attitude). Slide 8–81 is an example; slide 8–82 shows the four categories.

Ask the participants what causes might contribute to the symptom of the customer calling and complaining that none of the reports you sent were accurate.

Examples of possible answers the learners might give are

◆ **S**ystem: The program that prints the reports has a problem.

◆ **T**raining: The customer does not know how to read the reports.

◆ **E**nvironmental: The customer spent only five seconds looking at the reports.

◆ **M**otivation: The customer is angry about previous dealings with your department and is trying hard to make you look bad.

This model and practice will help people implement a thought process to carefully look past the obvious cause and consider multiple possibilities before deciding on what information needs to be used in determining the next action.

Learning Activity 10–18: Remembering

GOAL

The goal of this activity is to show the participants factors that influence memory and how to help people improve their ability to retain information.

MATERIALS

- ◆ blank paper for the participants
- ◆ PowerPoint slides 8–83 through 8–86

TIME

- ◆ 15 minutes

INSTRUCTIONS

Use PowerPoint slide 8–83 to make the transition into a discussion on customer presentations and meetings. Emphasize the wide variety of options available for presenting information. Ask learners to take a minute and memorize the list on slide 8–84. Move to slide 8–85 and ask them to ignore the slide for now and quickly write down what they remember from the previous slide on a blank piece of paper. You will use this exercise to demonstrate how memory works and to help people learn to leverage memory theory in their presentations.

Debrief using slide 8–85:

- ◆ **Primacy:** You remember the first thing (grass).

- ◆ **Recency:** You remember the last thing (carbon).

- ◆ **Different:** You remember something unique or out of place (Zulu).

- ◆ **Visual:** You remember in pictures (tree).

- ◆ **Emotion:** You remember something with an emotion attached (love).

- ◆ **Organization:** You remember by chunking like things together (paper, desk, pen, pencil, ruler, radio, carbon).

- ◆ **Context:** You remember things that "go together" in a context (truth, love, wisdom, meaning).

Ask for a show of hands from people who remembered *grass*—most will raise their hands. The most powerful memory driver is *primacy*—you remember the first thing that you hear, see, or do. Ask the learners how to leverage this in presentations; for example, always start with an agenda and don't waste time on long introductions.

Ask who remembered *carbon.* This probably will be fewer people, but you also don't know where they stopped when time was up. The theory of Recency says that we also remember the last thing. Ask them how to use this for presentations; for example, do a review at the end.

Ask who remembers *Zulu.* Ask the learners how the fact that people remember what is different can be used in presentations. Examples might be to vary the setting or use new facilitation techniques.

Ask people to share their strategy—emphasize the importance of the visual to some people (they associate words with the pictures in their minds). Others use context (bird and tree together) or other organization (things must be remembered in order). See how many people remembered the emotion-based words. These are more difficult for some participants because there is no picture to associate with them and they can be hard to put in context. Again, relate this to presentation skills by pointing out that visual people need slides or flipchart pages to help trigger their memories. Finish up the discussion with slide 8–86.

Learning Activity 10–19: Scenario Planning

GOAL

The goal of this activity is to help participants construct future-state scenarios to drive a strategic business plan.

MATERIALS

◆ PowerPoint slides 8–93, 8–94, and 8–95

TIME

◆ 15 minutes

INSTRUCTIONS

Slides 8–93 and 8–94 introduce the concept of Scenario Planning. It is irrational to think that we can create a Strategic Plan and anticipate the future, especially in today's world. Instead, Scenario Planning encourages us to create four possible futures and to build a strategy to avoid the ones we don't prefer or move toward the ones that we do prefer. The process, found on slide 8–95, is to take two important values, such as revenue and staff, and vary them over four possible futures.

Divide the class into four teams, and give them five minutes to describe how the people, processes, organizations, customers, services, and technology would be for their teams in the future (one future per team) for the four futures listed. Here's an example you can share with them:

> Revenue up, staff down: Staff has been cut to increase profit. Revenue is up because one of our products has become trendy. We have finally implemented new processes and technology so we can expand without adding people. Morale is finally growing, ... *and so on across the other aspects.*

Ask the class which future they would like to be in. Ask them to share where they are right now. Ask them to think about where their teams will go (which future) if nothing is done differently. The strategic plan would come after completing this kind of thinking—basically, it becomes just the implementation of a project plan to achieve the desired future and avoid those that are undesirable.

Learning Activity 10–20: Delphi Technique

GOAL

The goal of this activity is to implement a group technique that preserves anonymity of opinions but still encourages group creativity.

MATERIALS

- ◆ PowerPoint slide 8–100

- ◆ Handout 11–15: Delphi Technique Case Study

- ◆ clear plastic container of candy, with a note inside on which is written the number of pieces of candy in the container. The note must not be visible from the outside.

TIME

- ◆ 10 minutes

INSTRUCTIONS

Slide 8–100 introduces the Delphi Technique. This technique is good for anonymous participation and works well over email, although the activity here involves physical objects.

Distribute Handout 11–15: Delphi Technique Case Study (chapter 11, page 164). Explain that everyone needs to stay silent during this exercise. Pass the container of candy and ask each person to submit on a sticky note an estimate of how many pieces of candy are in the container (no discussion or questions). Ask for a volunteer with a calculator or computer to total the numbers as you write them on a flipchart page. Mark the High, Low, and Average counts.

Do this again, this time asking people to put their names on the notes as well as their guess. Give the candy to the person with the closest guess. Point out how the group started to polarize once the highs and lows came in. This exercise will usually demonstrate that the results tend to polarize if too many rounds are done.

Learning Activity 10–21: Nominal Group Technique

GOAL

The goal of this activity is to implement a group technique for managing conflict and uneven participation.

MATERIALS

- ◆ PowerPoint slide 8–101.

- ◆ Training Instrument 11–16: Nominal Group Technique Case Study

- ◆ a pen or some sort of distinctive item to serve as a "talking stick"

TIME

- ◆ 10 minutes

INSTRUCTIONS

Instruct the learners that they will each be given time to talk in her or his turn. During another's turn, no one else may talk or communicate nonverbally. During each person's time slot, he or she can either state his or her case or ask others questions. Go around twice, documenting views (answers to the case study) on a flipchart. Carefully enforce the very structured process. Explain that this technique can be useful when a meeting has fallen apart or you think there will be a great deal of conflict, but advise the participants to use this sparingly—it only works once in a while.

For a variation, help control the process by passing a "talking stick" (a pen or something else). Each person can talk only when they have the talking stick. Limit their time. Do two rounds.

The answer to the puzzle is 30: 1 4×4, 4 3×3, 9 2×2, 16 1×1

Learning Activity 10–22: Project Leadership

GOAL

The goal of this activity is to acquaint the participants with the basics of good project leadership.

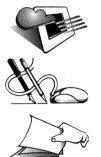

MATERIALS

- ◆ PowerPoint slides 8–102 through 8–112

- ◆ Training Instrument 11–18: Document Risk and Constraints

- ◆ Handouts 11–16 through 11–20

TIME

- ◆ 20 minutes

INSTRUCTIONS

Use slides 8–102 and 8–103 to introduce the concept of project leadership, in which all leaders must be well-versed. For more detail, review my book *Project Management for Trainers* listed in the Resources section. Distribute Handouts 11–16 through 11–20 (chapter 11, pages 165–168) for the learners' future reference.

Review slides 8–104 and 8–105, which help people understand how project management is different from their other leadership responsibilities, and review the roles of leader and team members using slide 8–106. Emphasize that the steps you will now show them are for the Define step, shown on slide 8–107, which is the part of projects most often skipped and most detrimental if skipped. Point out that it is important that they require project definition from the teams they lead.

Slide 8–108 shows the scope of a project. The squares represent the boundaries around the project—the source of the input and where the output goes. These rectangles represent the stakeholders—people who care, for many reasons, about a project. The project manager cannot control them but he or she must work hard to manage their expectations. These stakeholders can provide input to a project—such as requirements, constraints, expertise—or will receive output from a project, such as software or reports. The scope of the project is up to these stakeholders. Documenting the scope allows the right person—the project customer—to make the choice about whether to expand the scope (which will add cost or time).

Slide 8–109 shows a quick way to determine the risk of a project. Distribute Training Instrument 11–18: Document Risk and Constraints (chapter 11, page 197) and ask each learner to rank the riskiness of the size, structure, and technology for one of their projects. Emphasize that the higher the risk, the more time they must spend on project management. Through a show of hands, note the risk of the majority of their projects.

Slide 8–110 shows that only one of three aspects—time, cost, or quality—can be the top priority for the project. Quality can be exchanged for scope; in other words, if you are running out of time or money, you can either narrow the scope (a rational choice) or let the project turn out poorly (an irrational choice). Slides 8–111 and 8–112 demonstrate these choices.

Learning Activity 10–23: The Big Close

GOAL

The goal of this activity is to bring the program to an upbeat close.

MATERIALS

◆ A one-dollar bill

TIME

◆ 10 minutes

INSTRUCTIONS

I like to use the Dave Archer bill-folding trick to close. Ask everyone to take out paper money with a face on it (they all have faces on them). Explain to them that leadership is a choice—you can choose to grow your own leadership for success or you can choose to do nothing and live in dismay. Explain that you are going to leave them with something that will remind them that the choice is theirs alone.

Ask them to fold the bill at the edges of each side of the mouth (the first fold will almost be folding the bill in half). The final step is to make an additional fold the other way (like an accordion fold) in the middle of the mouth. The best way to do this is to squeeze the two other folds together.

Finally, ask the participants to loosen up the bill again and look at the face one more time. If they tilt it down, they will see a smiling face. If they tilt it up, they will see a sad face. Again, emphasize that the choice is theirs.

Handouts, Assessments, Training Instruments, and Tools

♦ Materials for supporting and enhancing the leadership training experience:

  ♦ 19 handouts

  ♦ 3 assessments

  ♦ 22 interactive training instruments

  ♦ 4 training tools

This chapter contains handouts, assessments, training instruments, and training tools that are used with the learning activities on leadership. Here is a list of the material in this chapter.

♦ Handout 11–1: The 10 Leadership Competencies

♦ Handout 11–2: Chuck's Role

♦ Handout 11–3: Angela's Role

♦ Handout 11–4: Observation Checklist

♦ Handout 11–5: A Difficult Conversations Checklist

♦ Handout 11–6: Adapting Your Style: Working with Core Style D

♦ Handout 11–7: Adapting Your Style: Working with Core Style I

♦ Handout 11–8: Adapting Your Style: Working with Core Style S

♦ Handout 11–9: Adapting Your Style: Working with Core Style C

♦ Handout 11–10: The Sabotage Exercise

♦ Handout 11–11: Team Member Assignment Cards for Sabotage

◆ Handout 11–12: Feedback

◆ Handout 11–13: Hints and Solutions for Feedback

◆ Handout 11–14: The Hero's Journey

◆ Handout 11–15: Delphi Technique Case Study

◆ Handout 11–16: Steps to Great Projects

◆ Handout 11–17: Define: Write the Project Definition

◆ Handout 11–18: Establish Project Scope

◆ Handout 11–19: What to Do if You're Behind

◆ Assessment 11–1: Leadership Self-Assessment

◆ Assessment 11–2: Quick n' Dirty DISC/PIAV Assessment (optional)

◆ Assessment 11–3: The Language System Diagnostic Instrument

◆ Training Instrument 11–1: Action Plan

◆ Training Instrument 11–2: Identification of Strengths and Weaknesses

◆ Training Instrument 11–3: Nine Dots

◆ Training Instrument 11–4: Practicing Flexibility: A Test of Your Creative Thinking Skills

◆ Training Instrument 11–5: Journaling: Resiliency

◆ Training Instrument 11–6: Journaling: Working with Others

◆ Training Instrument 11–7: Blending of Styles

◆ Training Instrument 11–8: Walk a Mile in My Shoes . . .

◆ Training Instrument 11–9: Journaling: Communication

◆ Training Instrument 11–10: Performance Review

◆ Training Instrument 11–11: Journaling: Coaching

◆ Training Instrument 11–12: Journaling: Vision

◆ Training Instrument 11–13: Change Versus Transition

◆ Training Instrument 11–14: Journaling: Change

◆ Training Instrument 11–15: Journaling: Customer Orientation

- ◆ Training Instrument 11–16: Nominal Group Technique Case Study

- ◆ Training Instrument 11–17: Journaling: Strategic Business Acumen

- ◆ Training Instrument 11–18: Document Risk and Constraints

- ◆ Training Instrument 11–19: Journaling: Project Leadership

- ◆ Training Instrument 11–20: Strength Worksheet

- ◆ Training Instrument 11–21: Opportunity Worksheet

- ◆ Training Instrument 11–22: Action Plan

- ◆ Tool 11–1: The Hero's Journey

- ◆ Tool 11–2: Systems Thinking

- ◆ Tool 11–3: Mini-Evaluation

- ◆ Tool 11–4: General Workshop Appraisal

Using the CD

The materials in this chapter also appear on the accompanying CD. You will find these items by inserting the CD and using the Adobe Acrobat software to open the .pdf files for the specific materials you wish to use in your training. When you locate the file(s) you need, simply print out the pages of the document(s) for your session.

Handout 11–1

The 10 Leadership Competencies

SELF-UNDERSTANDING: Self-Assessment
- Develop clarity of personal values, purpose, and vision
- Develop and execute a personal strategy
- Demonstrate authenticity through behavioral alignment with values and vision
- Take accountability for personal and leadership actions

SELF-UNDERSTANDING: Resiliency
- Be willing to jump in and get things started
- Seek opportunities for performance improvement and development
- Build on others' ideas for the benefit of the decision
- Maintain an appropriate, empowered attitude
- Persist in managing and overcoming adversity
- Act proactively in seeking new opportunities
- Prioritize tasks and manage time effectively

WORKING WITH OTHERS: Interpersonal and Relationship Skills
- Understand and appreciate diversity of perspective and style
- Participate and contribute fully as a team member
- Demonstrate empathy and understanding
- Build trust and demonstrate trustworthiness

WORKING WITH OTHERS: Communication Skills
- Understand and adapt to your audience to help others learn
- Express intention clearly and concisely in written communications
- Build collaboration and clearly articulate intention in verbal communications
- Have formal presentation skills
- Listen for understanding
- Manage flow of communication and information

WORKING WITH OTHERS: Employee Development (Coach and Motivate)
- Motivate employees to high performance.
- Coach for development and improved performance.
- Manage with appreciation and respect for diversity of individual values and needs.
- Delegate tasks as needed and with awareness of employee development opportunities.
- Select appropriate staff to fulfill specific project needs and responsibilities.

continued on next page

Handout 11–1, continued
The 10 Leadership Competencies

ALIGNMENT: Customer Orientation

- Understand and apply customer needs and expectations
- Gather customer requirements and input
- Partner with customers in gathering requirements, maintaining communication flow, and managing work
- Set and monitor performance standards

ALIGNMENT: Strategic Business Acumen

- Demonstrate ability to ethically build support for a perspective about which you feel strongly
- Think holistically in terms of the entire system and the effects and consequences of actions and decisions
- Operate with an awareness of marketplace competition and general landscape of related business arenas
- Have general business acumen in such functions as strategic planning, finance, marketing, manufacturing, and research and development

ALIGNMENT: Project Leadership

- Set, communicate, and monitor milestones and objectives
- Gain and maintain buy-in from sponsors and customers
- Prioritize and allocate resources
- Manage multiple, potentially conflicting priorities across various or diverse disciplines
- Maintain an effective, interactive, and productive team culture
- Manage budget and project progress
- Manage risk versus reward and ROI equations
- Balance established standards with need for exceptions in decision making
- Make timely decisions in alignment with customer and business pace

WORKING WITH OTHERS: Creating and Actualizing Vision

- Create a clear and inspirational vision of the desired outcome
- Align the vision with broader organizational strategies
- Translate the vision into manageable action steps
- Communicate vision to enroll or enlist staff, sponsors, and customers
- Influence and evangelize (sales, negotiation)
- Gather appropriate input
- Understand individual motivators and decision-making styles and use them to enroll others
- Facilitate win/win solutions

continued on next page

Handout 11–1, continued

The 10 Leadership Competencies

ALIGNMENT: Create, Support, and Manage Change

- ◆ Understand improvement Initiatives (three levels: managing your own transition and transformation, managing a corporate [external] change initiative, coaching others through transition)
- ◆ Identify and implement appropriate change initiatives and efforts
- ◆ Promote and build support for change initiatives
- ◆ Understand cost/benefit and return-on-investment of change initiatives
- ◆ Manage transition with employees. guiding and supporting the change process
- ◆ Support staff in navigating the transitional process and challenges through organizational change
- ◆ Demonstrate and build resilience in the face of change

Handout 11–2
Chuck's Role

You are **Chuck** and this is your story:

"I always try to finish my work on time, but last week I had flu and was worried it could be that anthrax thing because I opened a junk mail envelope from Florida. With all this terrorist business, I could not focus on my work and had to get some counseling. And all Angela did was yell at me for not finishing the tables for the monthly report. That woman is obsessed with trivial details. Nobody reads those reports anyhow and who cares if it is late by a couple of days?"

Handout 11–3
Angela's Role

You are **Angela** and this is your story:

"Chuck never finishes anything before the deadline. We both agree when his part of the task is to be completed but he is always late and always with a handy excuse. Last month his kid was sick. This month he had flu. He has my sympathy but I expect my coworkers to behave in a professional manner. He also complains that nobody reads the monthly reports anyhow, but it's not our job to make policy, is it?"

Handout 11–4

Observation Checklist

Instructions: From your perspective, what was the crux of this conflict? Write your observations in the spaces below.

1. Did Chuck and Angela seem more eager to talk or to listen?

2. What types of active listening behaviors did you notice?

3. What are some examples of negative behaviors and emotions (such as accusations, betrayal, domination, hostility, anger, frustration, and sarcasm) that you observed in the conversation between Chuck and Angela?

4. What are some examples of positive behaviors and emotions (such as understanding, apologizing, empathy, support, and hope) that you observed in the conversation between Chuck and Angela?

5. How did Chuck and Angela demonstrate their ability to use self-mediation techniques related to the following checklist items?

   ◆ Frame the session

   ◆ Gather information and analyze the conflict

   ◆ Establish mutual goals

   ◆ Brainstorm strategies for achieving the goals

   ◆ Select the best strategy

   ◆ Debrief

Handout 11–5
A Difficult Conversations Checklist

☐ **What Happened?**

- ◆ Where does your story come from? Facts? Past Experience? Rules? Theirs?
- ◆ What impact has this had on you?
- ◆ What might their objectives have been and how have you contributed to the problem?

☐ **Emotions**

- ◆ What are you really feeling? Why?

☐ **Identify**

- ◆ What's at stake for you about you?

☐ **Purposes**

- ◆ What do you hope to accomplish? Shift to support learning, sharing, problem solving.
- ◆ Is this the best way to address this issue?

☐ **Differences**

- ◆ Describe the problem in terms of the differences between your stories, and share the purpose.
- ◆ Invite them to join as a partner to solve the problem.

☐ **Explore the Stories**

- ◆ Listen to understand their viewpoint.
- ◆ Share your viewpoint.
- ◆ Reframe, reframe, reframe to keep on track.

☐ **Problem Solving**

- ◆ Invent options that meet each side's concerns.
- ◆ Look to standards for what should happen.
- ◆ Talk about how to keep communication open going forward.

Adapted from the book *Difficult Conversations* by Douglas Stone, Bruce Patton, and Sheila Heen.

Handout 11–6

Adapting Your Style: Working with Core Style D

BODY LANGUAGE:
- Keep your distance
- Strong handshake
- Lean forward
- Direct eye contact

TONE OF VOICE:
- Strong, clear, confident
- Direct
- Fast pace

ENERGIZERS:
- Challenges
- Opportunities to lead
- Tough assignments

DISSATISFIERS:
- Routine, mundane
- Lack of authority
- Lack of respect

WORDS/CONTENT:
- Win
- Lead the field
- Results
- Now, immediate
- Bottom line
- Challenge

DO'S AND DON'TS:
- Be clear, specific, and to the point
- Stick to business
- Be prepared and packaged
- Provide alternative choices
- Take issue with the facts, not the person
- Let it be their idea
- Don't waste time
- Present facts logically
- Ask specific "what" questions
- Don't offer guarantees you can't keep
- Provide a win/win opportunity

Handout 11–7

Adapting Your Style: Working with Core Style I

BODY LANGUAGE:
- Get close
- Sit next to
- Smile, relax, have fun
- Friendly eye contact
- Expressive gestures

TONE OF VOICE:
- Enthusiastic
- Modulations
- Persuasive, colorful
- Fast pace

ENERGIZERS:
- People interactions
- Social recognition
- Inspiration

DISSATISFIERS:
- Social rejection
- Skepticism
- Negativity

WORDS/CONTENT:
- Fun
- I feel
- Socialize, recognition
- Exciting
- Picture this
- People

DO'S AND DON'TS
- Support their dreams
- Talk about people and their goals
- Ask for opinion
- Provide ideas for implementing actions
- Don't talk down
- Allow time for socializing
- Don't drive for facts, figures
- Put details in writing
- Provide testimonials— "important" people
- Offer incentives for risks
- Make them feel special

Handout 11–8

Adapting Your Style: Working with Core Style S

BODY LANGUAGE:
- ◆ Relaxed, calm
- ◆ Methodical
- ◆ Lean back, don't rush
- ◆ Friendly eye contact
- ◆ Small gestures

TONE OF VOICE:
- ◆ Warm, soft, calm
- ◆ Steady
- ◆ Low tone, volume
- ◆ Slow pace

ENERGIZERS:
- ◆ Defined territory, security
- ◆ Closure
- ◆ Team Harmony
- ◆ Opportunity to serve

DISSATISFIERS:
- ◆ Loss of security
- ◆ Lack of closure
- ◆ Surprises
- ◆ No "home" base

WORDS/CONTENT:
- ◆ Step-by-step
- ◆ Help me out
- ◆ Guarantee, promise
- ◆ Think about it, take your time

DO'S AND DON'TS:
- ◆ Start with personal connection
- ◆ Listen!
- ◆ Present your point logically, nonthreateningly
- ◆ Look for hurt feelings
- ◆ Don't mistake willingness for agreement
- ◆ Provide information
- ◆ Show interest in them as individuals
- ◆ Don't force a quick response—patience
- ◆ Don't interrupt
- ◆ Provide personal assurances/guarantee
- ◆ Allow time to think/make decisions

Handout 11–9

Adapting Your Style: Working with Core Style C

BODY LANGUAGE:
- Keep your distance
- Sit across from
- Firm posture
- Direct eye contact
- Little/no hand gestures

TONE OF VOICE:
- Controlled, direct
- Thoughtful, precise
- Little modulations
- Slow pace

ENERGIZERS:
- Information
- Quality standards
- Compliance with rules
- Analysis, research

DISSATISFIERS:
- Personal criticism
- Moving too fast
- Decisions without data
- Irrational feelings/emotions

WORDS/CONTENT:
- Here are the facts
- The data show
- Proven
- Take your time, no risk
- Analyze
- Guarantees

DO'S AND DON'TS:
- Prepare your case
- Approach in straightforward way
- Provide policies/rules to follow
- Give time for decisions
- Be conservative, don't overpromise
- Prove with facts
- Loyalty
- Don't be disorganized
- Don't be casual, informal, or personal
- Build credibility—look at all sides
- Present specifics
- Take time, but be persistent
- Help them do things "right"
- Be fair and consistent

Handout 11–10

The Sabotage Exercise

Purpose: To explore how the lack of trust affects team productivity

Order: ◆ ♥ ♣ ♠

> *Two through Ace*
>
> *Face up (two of diamonds on top of stack)*
>
> *No jokers*

Instructions: You will be divided into teams and each team will be given a shuffled deck of cards. Your job is to arrange the cards in the correct order and give the deck to the monitor on your team. If the arrangement is correct, your team will receive a point, and another shuffled deck for processing. The team with the highest number of points at the end of a five-minute period will win fabulous merchandise.

Prior to the production period, all teams will have a five-minute planning period.

Some teams will have a saboteur in their midst who will try to reduce team productivity. During the planning period, the saboteur may make inappropriate suggestions, ask irrelevant questions, and try to confuse and irritate others. During the production period, the saboteur may slow down the process, lose a card, or misplace a card.

If you are selected as a saboteur, it is important that you work in a sneaky fashion. If you are not caught, you will win fabulous merchandise!

Handout 11–11

Team Member Assignment Cards for the Sabotage Exercise

You belong to Team B.
Your team **does have**
a saboteur but you
don't know who it is.

You belong to Team D.
Your team **does not have**
any saboteurs.

You are a saboteur.
You belong to Team B.
Your teammates **know** they
have a saboteur in their midst
but they **do not know** it is you.

You are a saboteur.
You belong to Team D.
Your teammates **do not know**
they have a saboteur
in their midst.

You belong to Team A.
Your team **does not have**
any saboteurs.

You belong to Team C.
Your team **does have**
a saboteur but you
don't know who it is.

continued on next page

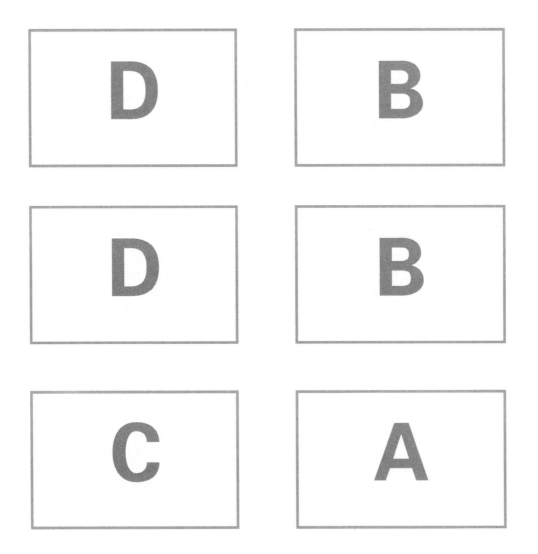

Handout 11–12

Feedback

Instructions: Each of these is a sentence cut up into three-character chunks (including the spaces and punctuation marks). The team member has five minutes to solve these three puzzles with the leader's help. Hints are on the next page, but only the leader can look at them. Also, the solutions are on the following page. Again, only the leader can look at them.

Chunks 1

(DO) (FL) (JU) (DON) (EE,) (FIG) (FLO) (HT,) (N'T) (ST) ('T) (W!)

Chunks 2

(EV) (WI) (WI) (A C) (ERY) (ESS) (IN) (LIC) (NO) (NS) (NS!) (ONE) (ONE) (ONF) (T,) (UNL)

Chunks 3

(AR) (EA) (PR) (TH) (. Y) (CAN) (CON) (CT) (CTS) (E L) (EDI) (EM.) (ENT) (FLI) (IKE) (KES) (M O) (NOT) (OU) (QUA) (R P) (REV) (RTH) (THE)

Handout 11–13

Hints and Solutions for Feedback

HINTS

- ◆ **Chunks 1:** The first word is "Don't."

- ◆ **Chunks 2:** One of the words is "unless."

- ◆ **Chunks 3:** The last word is "them."

SOLUTIONS

- ◆ **Chunks 1:** Don't fight, don't flee, just flow!

- ◆ **Chunks 2:** In a conflict, no one wins unless everyone wins!

- ◆ **Chunks 3:** Conflicts are like earthquakes. You cannot predict them or prevent them.

Handout 11–14

The Hero's Journey

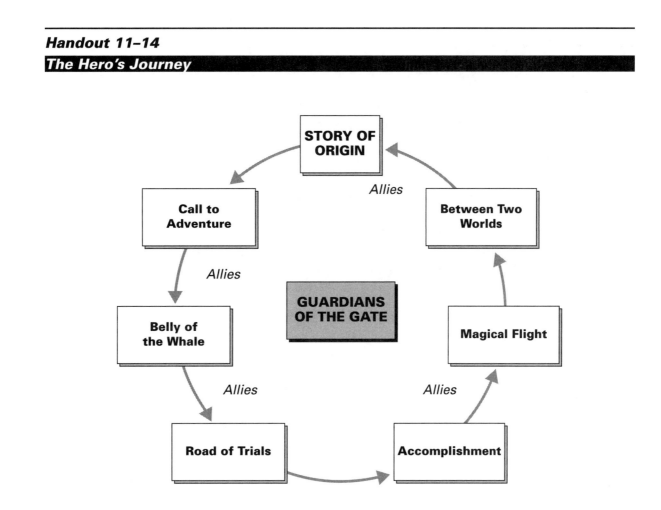

Handout 11–15
Delphi Technique Case Study

Instructions: In this case study we will practice implementing the Delphi Technique. Your instructor will show you a jar of candy. Please do the following things:

- ◆ Appoint a facilitator for your group.
- ◆ Ask each person to guess how many pieces of candy are in the jar, to write down his or her guess, and to submit it to the facilitator. The facilitator should average the guesses and then communicate this (and the high and low) to the group. There should be NO discussion.
- ◆ Repeat this process three times. At the end of three cycles, discuss what might have been the outcome if there had been more cycles of guessing.

Handout 11–16
Steps to Great Projects

Dare to Properly Manage Resources!

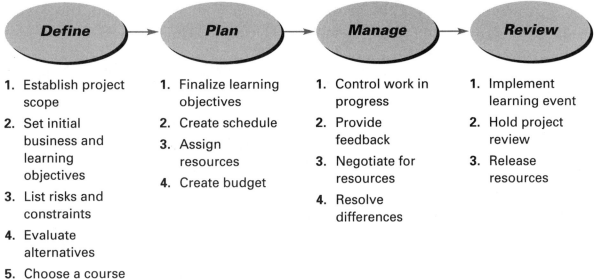

Define

1. Establish project scope
2. Set initial business and learning objectives
3. List risks and constraints
4. Evaluate alternatives
5. Choose a course of action

Plan

1. Finalize learning objectives
2. Create schedule
3. Assign resources
4. Create budget

Manage

1. Control work in progress
2. Provide feedback
3. Negotiate for resources
4. Resolve differences

Review

1. Implement learning event
2. Hold project review
3. Release resources

Handout 11–17

Define: Write the Project Definition

PROJECT DEFINITION

- ◆ Scope

- ◆ Objectives (goals, specifications)

- ◆ Risk

- ◆ Constraints

- ◆ Alternatives

- ◆ Course of Action

Handout 11–18
Establish Project Scope

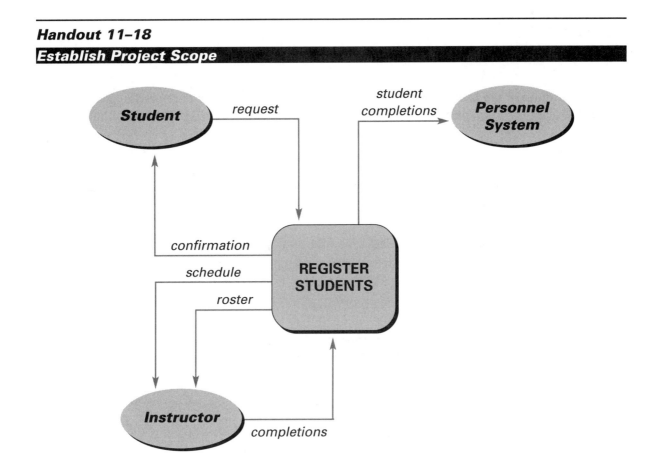

Handout 11–19

What to Do if You're Behind

Explanation of the table: The **X**s in the Cost or Schedule columns denote that taking that particular action will affect the project's budget, timeline, or both.

ACTION	COST	SCHEDULE
1. **Renegotiate:** Discuss with your client the prospect of increasing the budget for the project or extending the deadline for completion.	X	X
2. **Recover During Later Steps:** If you begin to fall behind in early steps of a project, re-examine budgets and schedules for later steps. Perhaps you can save on later steps so the overall budget and/or schedule is met.	X	X
3. **Narrow Project Scope:** Perhaps nonessential elements of the project can be eliminated, thereby reducing costs and/or saving time.	X	X
4. **Deploy More Resources:** You may need to put more people or machines on the project to meet a critical schedule. Increased costs must be weighed against the importance of the deadline.		X
5. **Accept Substitution:** When something is not available or is more expensive than budgeted, substituting a comparable item may solve your problem.	X	X
6. **Seek Alternative Sources:** When a supplier can't deliver within budget or schedule, look for others who can. (You may choose to accept a substitute rather than seek other sources.)	X	X
7. **Accept Partial Delivery:** Sometimes a supplier can deliver a partial order to keep your project on schedule and complete the delivery later.		X
8. **Offer Incentives:** Go beyond the scope of the original contract and offer a bonus or other incentive for on-time delivery.		X
9. **Demand Compliance:** Sometimes demanding that people do what they agreed to do gets the desired results. You may have to appeal to higher management for backing and support.	X	X

Assessment 11–1
Leadership Self-Assessment

Instructions: For each bulleted subcompetency, rate your own strength by marking **H** (high), **M** (medium), or **L** (low). After you have rated each of the bulleted items, return to the competency and give yourself an overall rating (high, medium, or low).

Inner Work: Self-Awareness　　　　　　　　　　　　　　　　RATING: _____

◆ Develop clarity of personal values, purpose, and vision.　　RATING: _____

◆ Develop and execute a personal branding strategy.　　　　RATING: _____

◆ Demonstrate authenticity through behavioral alignment with values and vision.　　　　　　　　　　　　　　　　RATING: _____

◆ Take accountability for personal and leadership actions.　　RATING: _____

◆ Know and trust your own intuition.　　　　　　　　　　RATING: _____

◆ Learn to learn: new technology.　　　　　　　　　　　RATING: _____

Inner Work: Resiliency　　　　　　　　　　　　　　　　　RATING: _____

◆ Be willing to jump in and get things started.　　　　　　RATING: _____

◆ Seek opportunities for performance improvement and development.　　　　　　　　　　　　　　　　　　RATING: _____

◆ Build on others' ideas for the benefit of the decision.　　RATING: _____

◆ Maintain appropriate, empowered attitude.　　　　　　RATING: _____

◆ Persistence in managing and overcoming adversity.　　RATING: _____

◆ Act proactively in seeking new opportunities.　　　　　RATING: _____

◆ Prioritize tasks and manage time.　　　　　　　　　　RATING: _____

Working with Others (Managers, Subordinates, Peers): Interpersonal and Relationship Skills　　　　　　　　RATING: _____

◆ Understand and appreciate diversity of perspective and style.　RATING: _____

◆ Participate and contribute fully as a team member.　　RATING: _____

◆ Demonstrate empathy and understanding.　　　　　　RATING: _____

◆ Build trust and demonstrate trustworthiness.　　　　　RATING: _____

Working with Others (Managers, Subordinates, Peers): Communication Skills　　　　　　　　　　　　　　RATING: _____

◆ Understand and adapt to your audience, helping others to learn.　RATING: _____

◆ Express intention clearly and concisely in written communications.　RATING: _____

◆ Build collaboration and clearly articulate intention in verbal communications.　　　　　　　　　　　　　　　RATING: _____

◆ The formal presentation skills.　　　　　　　　　　　RATING: _____

◆ Listen for understanding.　　　　　　　　　　　　　RATING: _____

◆ Manage flow of communication/information.　　　　　RATING: _____

continued on next page

Assessment 11–1, continued
Leadership Self-Assessment

Working with Others (Managers, Subordinates, Peers): Employee Development (Coach and Motivate)   **RATING:** _____

- Motivate employees to high performance.   **RATING:** _____
- Coach for development and improved performance.   **RATING:** _____
- Manage with appreciation and respect for diversity of individual values and needs.   **RATING:** _____
- Delegate tasks as needed and with awareness of employee development opportunities.   **RATING:** _____
- Select appropriate staff to fulfill specific project needs and responsibilities.   **RATING:** _____

Working with Others (External): Customer Orientation   **RATING:** _____

- Understand and apply customer needs and expectations.   **RATING:** _____
- Gather customer requirements and input.   **RATING:** _____
- Partner with customer in gathering requirements, maintaining communication flow, and managing work.   **RATING:** _____
- Set and monitor performance standards.   **RATING:** _____

Working with Others (External): Strategic Business Acumen   **RATING:** _____

- Demonstrate ability to ethically build support for a perspective about which you feel strongly.   **RATING:** _____
- Think holistically in terms of the entire system and the effects and consequences of actions and decisions.   **RATING:** _____
- Operate with an awareness of marketplace competition and general landscape of related business arenas.   **RATING:** _____
- Has general business acumen in such functions as strategic planning, finance, marketing, manufacturing, and research and development.   **RATING:** _____

Working with Others (External): Project Leadership   **RATING:** _____

- Build cohesive teams with shared purpose and high performance.   **RATING:** _____
- Set, communicate, and monitor milestones and objectives.   **RATING:** _____
- Gain and maintain buy-in from sponsors and customers.   **RATING:** _____
- Prioritize and allocate resources.   **RATING:** _____
- Manage multiple, potentially conflicting priorities across various/diverse disciplines.   **RATING:** _____
- Create and define systems and processes to translate vision into action.   **RATING:** _____
- Maintain an effective, interactive, and productive team culture.   **RATING:** _____

continued on next page

Assessment 11–1, continued
Leadership Self-Assessment

◆ Manage budget and project progress. RATING: _____

◆ Gather and analyze appropriate data and input and manage "noise" of information overload. RATING: _____

◆ Manage risk versus reward and return-on-investment equations. RATING: _____

◆ Balance established standards with need for exceptions in decision making. RATING: _____

◆ Align decisions with needs of business and with organization and team values. RATING: _____

◆ Make timely decisions in alignment with customer and business pace. RATING: _____

Working with Others (External): Creating and Actualizing Vision RATING: _____

◆ Create a clear and inspirational vision of the desired outcome. RATING: _____

◆ Align the vision with broader organizational strategies. RATING: _____

◆ Translate the vision into manageable action steps. RATING: _____

◆ Communicate vision to enroll and enlist staff, sponsors, and customers. RATING: _____

◆ Influence and evangelize (sales, negotiation). RATING: _____

◆ Gather appropriate input. RATING: _____

◆ Understand individual motivators and decision-making styles and use them to enroll others. RATING: _____

◆ Facilitate win/win solutions. RATING: _____

The Challenge of Change: Create, Support, and Manage Change RATING: _____

◆ Understand improvement Initiatives (three levels: managing your own transition/transformation, managing a corporate (external) change initiative, coaching others through transition) RATING: _____

◆ Identify and implement appropriate change initiatives/efforts. RATING: _____

◆ Promote and build support for change initiatives. RATING: _____

◆ Understand cost/benefit and return-on-investment of change initiatives. RATING: _____

◆ Manage transition with employees, guiding and supporting the change process. RATING: _____

◆ Support staff in navigating transitional process and challenges through organizational change. RATING: _____

◆ Demonstrate and build resilience in the face of change. RATING: _____

Assessment 11–2
Quick n' Dirty DISC/PIAV Assessment

Instructions: On these two pages, circle any words (as many as you want) that sound like descriptions of you.

Dominance, Influences, Steadiness, and Compliance (DISC)

C		D
	Careful	
	Objective, clear	Urgent
	High standards	Pioneering
	Good analyst	Innovative
	Detailed	Driven
	Picky	Likes challenges
	Aloof	Demanding
	Fearful	Quick to anger

S		I
	Steady and sincere	Optimistic
	Patient	Motivator
	Empathic	Team player
	Logical	Problem solver
	Service oriented	Emotionally needy
	Apathetic under stress	Inattentive
	Passive	Trusting
	Resists change	Poor with details

continued on next page

Assessment 11–2, continued

Quick n' Dirty DISC/PIAV Assessment

TRADITIONAL

Search for value of life

Champion of beliefs

Rigid

Order, unity

Always right

SOCIAL

Help others

Empathy

Generous

Self-sacrifice

Can't say "no"

Stop hate and conflict

THEORETICAL

Seeks truth/ knowledge

Problem solving

Impractical

Watches Discovery
Channel, PBS

AESTHETIC

Achieve inner vision

Self-fulfillment

Humor or sarcasm

Impractical

Inner feelings, not logic

INDIVIDUALISTIC

Seeks to win

Control, power

End justifies means

Breaks rules

Can appear to
feel superior to others

UTILITARIAN

Make money

Practical

Future-oriented, savings

Workaholic

Never enough

Assessment 11–3
The Language System Diagnostic Instrument

Part One

Instructions: This instrument contains three parts. Part One consists of five sets of three paragraphs each. For each set, pick your favorite paragraph. Do not be concerned with the actual content of the paragraph, merely with how you respond to it compared with the other paragraphs in the set. Read all three paragraphs and then make your selection, but do not deliberate too long; your first response generally is best. Indicate the letter of the paragraph that you have selected on your answer sheet by circling the appropriate letter (**A, B,** or **C**) for each set.

You have five minutes in which to complete the entire instrument.

1. **A.** The tinkle of the wind chimes tells me that the breeze is still rustling outside. In the distance, I can hear the whistle of the train.

   B. I can see the rows of flowers in the yard, their colors shining and fading in the sunlight and shadows, their petals waving in the breeze.

   C. As I ran, I could feel the breeze on my back. My feet pounded along the path. The blood raced through my veins and I felt very alert.

2. **A.** I like to be warm. On a cold night, I like to relax by a warm fire in a comfortable room with a cup of smooth, warm cocoa and a fuzzy blanket.

   B. The child talked into the toy telephone as though he were calling a friend. Listening to the quiet conversation, I could almost hear the echoes of another child, long ago.

   C. The view was magnificent. It was one of the most beautiful things I have ever seen. The panorama of the green countryside stretched out clearly below us in the bright, sparkling sun.

3. **A.** They appeared to be surprised when they noticed that there were other people on the beach. The amazement on their faces turned to eagerness as they looked to see if they knew any of the people on the sand.

   B. I was helped up and supported until I felt my strength coming back. The tingling sensation that ran up and down my legs—especially in my calves—was stronger after I stood up, and my body was extremely warm.

   C. People will express themselves more verbally if they can talk about their interests or assets. You can hear the increased enthusiasm in their conversations.

4. **A.** The feedback that the speaker received was an indication that she was communicating more effectively. The people in the audience seemed to be in tune with what she was talking about.

   B. I want to understand how people feel in their inner worlds, to accept them as they are, to create an atmosphere in which they feel free to think and feel and be anything they desire.

   C. Children watch adults. They notice more than we realize. You can see this if you observe them at play. They mimic the behavior of the grown-ups they see.

continued on next page

Assessment 11–3, continued
The Language System Diagnostic Instrument

5. **A.** Creative, artistic people have an eye for beauty. They see patterns and forms that other people do not notice. They respond to the colors around them, and their visual surrounding can affect their moods.

   B. They heard the music as if for the first time. Each change of tone and tempo caught their ears. The sounds soared throughout the room, while the rhythms echoed in their heads.

   C. Everybody was stirred by the deep emotions generated by the interaction. Some felt subdued and experienced it quietly. Others were stimulated and excited. They all felt alert to each new sensation.

Part Two

Instructions: This part consists of ten sets of items. Each item includes three lists (sets) of words. For each item, circle the letter (**A, B,** or **C**) of your favorite set of words. Do not focus on the meanings of the words. Try to work quickly.

6. **A.** Witness Look See	**B.** Interview Listen Hear	**C.** Sensation Touch Feel
7. **A.** Stir Sensitive Hustle	**B.** Watch Scope Pinpoint	**C.** Squeal Remark Discuss
8. **A.** Proclaim Mention Acoustic	**B.** Texture Handle Tactile	**C.** Exhibit Inspect Vista
9. **A.** Scrutinize Focused Scene	**B.** Articulate Hearken Tone	**C.** Exhilarate Support Grip
10. **A.** Ringing Hearsay Drumbeat	**B.** Movement Heat Rushing	**C.** Glitter Mirror Outlook
11. **A.** Dream Glow Illusion	**B.** Firm Quiet Silence	**C.** Bright Soft Tender
12. **A.** Upbeat Listen Record	**B.** Firm Hold Concrete	**C.** Bright Appear Picture
13. **A.** Feeling Lukewarm Muscle	**B.** Hindsight Purple Book	**C.** Hearsay Audible Horn

continued on next page

Assessment 11–3, continued
The Language System Diagnostic Instrument

14. **A.** Show   **B.** Tempo   **C.** Glowing
       Observant   Articulate   Lookout
       Glimpse   Sonar   Vision

15. **A.** Purring   **B.** Smooth   **C.** Glowing
       Overhear   Grasp   Lookout
       Melody   Relaxed   Vision

Part Three

Instructions: This part consists of ten sets of three short phrases each. In each set, circle the letter (**A, B,** or **C**) of your favorite phrase. Complete this task in the time remaining.

16. **A.** An eyeful   **B.** An earful   **C.** A handful
17. **A.** Lend me an ear   **B.** Give him a hand   **C.** Keep an eye out
18. **A.** Hand in hand   **B.** Eye to eye   **C.** Word for word
19. **A.** Get the picture   **B.** Hear the word   **C.** Come to grips with
20. **A.** The thrill of the chase   **B.** A flash of lightning   **C.** The roll of thunder
21. **A.** Outspoken   **B.** Underhanded   **C.** Short-sighted
22. **A.** I see   **B.** I hear you   **C.** I get it
23. **A.** Hang in there   **B.** Bird's-eye view   **C.** Rings true
24. **A.** Clear as a bell   **B.** Smooth as silk   **C.** Bright as day
25. **A.** Look here   **B.** Listen up   **C.** Catch this

Scoring and Interpretation begin on next page

Assessment 11–3, continued
The Language System Diagnostic Instrument

Scoring and Interpretation

1. Transfer your responses from the LSDI to this sheet by circling the letter that you chose for each of the numbered items on the preceding three pages.

Part One: Paragraphs

1.	A	B	C
2.	B	C	A
3.	C	A	B
4.	A	C	B
5.	B	A	C

Part Two: Words

6.	B	A	C
7.	C	B	A
8.	A	C	B
9.	B	A	C
10.	A	C	B
11.	B	A	C
12.	A	C	B
13.	C	B	A
14.	B	A	C
15.	A	C	B

Part Three: Phrases

16.	B	A	C
17.	A	C	B
18.	C	B	A
19.	B	A	C
20.	C	B	A
21.	A	C	B
22.	B	A	C
23.	C	B	A
24.	A	C	B
25.	B	A	C
Totals	I_____	II_____	III_____

continued on next page

Assessment 11–3, continued
The Language System Diagnostic Instrument

2. Now, total the letters circled in each vertical column. Place the three scores from Columns I, II, III on the lines below, and multiply each of the column scores by 4, as indicated, to determine the actual score.

Actual Scores

Column I _____ × 4 = _____ (Actual Score)

Column II _____ × 4 = _____ (Actual Score)

Column III _____ × 4 = _____ (Actual Score)

3. Chart your actual scores below, making a horizontal bar graph by coloring in each row to the point that represents your actual score in each of the three columns.

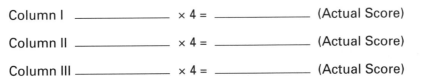

4. Your highest score indicates the **primary** mode that you use to interpret and communicate with the world around you. You probably use this mode (auditory, visual, or kinesthetic) the most, particularly when you are problem solving or in a stressful situation.

Your second highest (middle) score indicates your **secondary** mode, which you likely use in everyday conversation, in combination with your primary mode.

Your lowest score indicates your **tertiary** mode, which you may not use as much as the other two, or may not use at all in your normal conversation. In fact, it often remains at the unconscious level.

These three modes of perceiving and talking about one's experiences are called "language representational systems." A visual person is likely to say, "I see," or, "That looks right." A kinesthetic person is more likely to say, "I've got it," or, "That feels right," whereas an auditory person might say, "I hear you," or, "That sounds right."

Each individual seems to be most comfortable using one or two of these systems. Some people believe, however, that learning to communicate in all three systems might lead a person to increased effectiveness in communication.

Developed by Cresencio Torres.

Training Instrument 11–1

Action Plan

Instructions: In the spaces below, identify your leadership strengths and weaknesses.

◆ I believe that my greatest leadership strengths are:

◆ Others believe that my greatest leadership strengths are:

◆ I believe that I need to develop the following leadership competencies:

◆ Others believe that I need to develop the following leadership competencies:

◆ I choose to create a strategy for working with others for this competency (instead of growing it myself):

Training Instrument 11–2
Identification of Strengths and Weaknesses

Instructions: In the spaces below, identify your leadership strengths and weaknesses.

◆ I believe that my greatest leadership strengths are:

◆ Others believe that my greatest leadership strengths are:

◆ I believe that I need to develop the following leadership competencies:

◆ Others believe that I need to develop the following leadership competencies:

◆ I choose to create a strategy for working with others for this competency (instead of growing it myself):

Training Instrument 11–3
Nine Dots

Instructions: Cover the lower half of this page with a sheet of paper. Connect the nine dots below without lifting your pen or pencil from the page. Then remove the cover sheet and turn the page upside down to check your solution against the puzzle's answer.

Practicing Flexibility: Adopting new ways of seeing and thinking

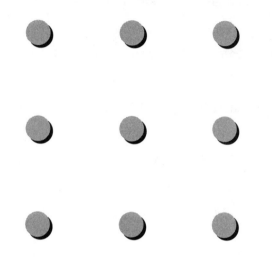

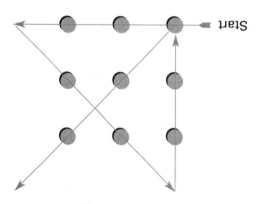

Training Instrument 11–4
Practicing Flexibility: A Test of Your Creative Thinking Skills

Instructions: Answer the following questions.

1. Do they have a Fourth of July in England?

2. How many birthdays does the average man have?

3. Some months have 31 days; how many have 28?

4. How many outs are there in an inning?

5. Is it legal for a man in California to marry his widow's sister?

6. Divide 30 by 1/2 and add 10. What is the answer?

7. If there are three apples and you take away two, how many do you have?

8. A doctor gives you three pills telling you to take one every half hour. How many minutes would the pills last?

9. A farmer has 17 sheep, and all but 9 die. How many are left?

10. How many animals of each sex did Moses take on the ark?

11. A clerk in the butcher shop is 5' 10" tall. What does he weigh?

12. How many two-cent stamps are there in a dozen?

Answers appear on next page

Training Instrument 11–4, continued

Answers to the Test of Your Creative Thinking Skills

1. Yes, it comes after the third of July!

2. Just one—the day he is born.

3. Twelve, all of them have at least 28 days

4. Six! Three per side!

5. No—if he has a widow, he's dead!

6. Seventy (30 divided by .5 equals 60!)

7. Two. You took them, remember?

8. Sixty. Start with the first pill, 30 minutes later take the second, then 30 minutes after that take the third.

9. Nine. If 8 out of 17 die, all but 9 die, eh?

10. Zero. Moses didn't have an ark, Noah did!

11. Meat—a butcher weighs meat!

12. Twelve. There are 12 two-cent stamps in a dozen!

Scoring

Number correct:

12	Creative Genius
10–11	Above Normal Creativity
7–9	Normal
4–6	You must need a cup of coffee.
1–3	That must have been some party last night!
0	Is there any next of kin you would like us to notify?

Training Instrument 11–5
Journaling: Resiliency

Instructions: Use the space below to complete or respond to the statements.

- ◆ I am resilient when I practice this personal strength I currently have:

- ◆ I would like to grow more resilient by working on:

- ◆ Here are five ways I plan to "eddy out":

- ◆ Here are ways I can leverage my strengths to help my team be more resilient:

Training Instrument 11–6
Journaling: Working with Others

Instructions: Use the space below to complete or respond to the statements.

♦ The behavioral strengths I am most comfortable with are:

♦ The behaviors that are the biggest challenge for me are:

♦ The following things motivate me:

♦ The following motivators I find distasteful in others:

♦ A significant relationship that will require me to adapt is:

♦ I will adapt by:

♦ I will improve the way I manage conflict by:

Training Instrument 11–7
Blending of Styles

Instructions: This chart is a worksheet for thinking through how different (or similar) styles blend. In the Work Relationship column, choose Good, Fair, or Poor. Next fill in the strengths and limitations of the relationship in the next two columns. Finally, suggest how the people could adapt to improve their relationship. For example, remember that a strong D behavior focuses on tasks and speed whereas a strong S behavior focuses on people and diligence. That relationship is poor because the approach they take in working with others or is problem solving—each one's behavioral preference—is opposite on both dimensions.

BLENDING OF STYLES	WORK RELATIONSHIP (GOOD/FAIR/POOR)	STRENGTHS OF THIS RELATIONSHIP	LIMITATIONS OF THIS RELATIONSHIP	ADAPTATIONS REQUIRED FOR OPTIMAL SUCCESS
D and D				
D and I				
D and S				
D and C				
I and I				
I and S				
I and C				
S and S				
S and C				
C and C				

Training Instrument 11–8

Walk a Mile in My Shoes...

Scenario 1

Budget time—every year your company is asked to budget for the next fiscal year. The budget process starts in the summer and concludes in early fall with a comprehensive strategic plan and budget presentation to Corporate. To prepare for the budget presentation, each of the functions must present goals, priorities, staffing needs, and budget requests.

Every year it seems that we submit out department's budget and the corporate office gives us back a dollar amount less than what we asked for. We then have to live with that number and figure out how to either increase our revenue or reduce our spending. It always seems to result in conflicts between functions on who gets to spend what and which initiatives or staffing plans get cut.

Given your selected STYLE and VALUE:

1. Share your reactions to this process with your peer.
2. Discuss a way to work within this inevitable budgeting process.

Scenario 2

Budgetary constraints have led to a reduction in the number of contractors retained for this year. However, the number of services offered by your department has stayed the same. All staff, therefore, have been given an increased work load. Some complaints have been lodged by staff who feel they are doing work beyond what they are able to handle.

Chris, a staff member who has been employed there for several years, was overheard telling a customer that the quality he was able to offer them was being traded for a few extra dollars of profit.

Choose one of you to be "Chris" and the other "Chris's Manager." Share your reactions to the situation:

1. Role-play an exchange between Chris and the Manager.
2. Debrief how your styles and your values blended or conflicted.
3. How could each of you adapt to improve this communication?
4. What would change about this interaction if you switched roles?

Training Instrument 11–9

Journaling: Communication

Instructions: Use the space below to complete or respond to the statements.

◆ I communicate best when I practice this personal strength I currently have:

◆ I would like to grow my ability to communicate by working on:

◆ Here are three ways I plan to improve my communication:

◆ Here are ways I can leverage my strengths to help my team communicate more effectively:

Training Instrument 11–10
Performance Review

Instructions: Answer the questions below by placing a checkmark in the appropriate box.

	NO	YES
◆ Did you discuss each goal or objective established for this employee?	☐	☐
◆ Are you and the employee clear on the areas of agreement? Disagreement?	☐	☐
◆ Did you and the employee cover all positive skills, traits, accomplishments, areas of growth, etc.? Did you reinforce the employee's accomplishments?	☐	☐
◆ Did you give the employee a sense of what you thought of his or her potential or ability?	☐	☐
◆ Are you both clear on areas where improvement is required? Expected? Demanded? Desired?	☐	☐
◆ What training or development recommendations did you agree on?	☐	☐
◆ Did you indicate consequences for noncompliance, if appropriate?	☐	☐
◆ Did you set good objectives for the next appraisal period?	☐	☐
Objective?	☐	☐
Specific?	☐	☐
Measurable?	☐	☐
◆ Standard to be used for evaluation?	☐	☐
Timeframe?	☐	☐
◆ Did you set a time for the next evaluation?	☐	☐
◆ Did you confirm what your part would be? Did the employee confirm his or her part?	☐	☐
◆ Did you thank the employee for his or her efforts?	☐	☐

Training Instrument 11–11

Journaling: Coaching

Instructions: Use the space below to complete or respond to the statements.

◆ I am an effective coach when I practice this personal strength I currently have:

◆ I would like to grow my coaching ability by working on:

◆ Here are two people I would like to coach more effectively:

◆ Here are ways I can leverage my strengths to help these two people meet their personal and business goals:

Training Instrument 11–12
Journaling: Vision

Instructions: Use the space below to complete or respond to the statements.

◆ I can leverage my personal vision by:

◆ I would like to grow a more clear and shared vision with my team by:

◆ Here are five places I need to reinforce and actualize the team vision:

◆ Here are ways I can continuously model our team vision:

Training Instrument 11–13
Change Versus Transition

Instructions: Draw a circle around those words/phrases that are a part of change, and draw a box around those that are part of transition.

PROCESS

EXTERNAL

SITUATION

INTERNAL

DECISION

IDENTITY

ADAPTATION

STATE OF MIND

DISRUPTION

CIRCUMSTANCE

Training Instrument 11–14
Journaling: Change

Instructions: Use the space below to complete or respond to the statements.

◆ I help others manage change when I practice this personal strength I currently have:

◆ I would like to grow my ability to help others with change by working on:

◆ Here are three changes I see coming up and my strategy:

◆ Here are ways I can leverage my strengths to help my team deal more effectively with change:

Training Instrument 11–15
Journaling: Customer Orientation

Instructions: Use the space below to complete or respond to the statements.

◆ My customers and the service I provide to them are:

◆ I would like to grow and define my team's customer service by:

◆ Here are five ways I plan to be more customer oriented personally:

◆ Here are ways I can leverage my strengths to help my team be more customer oriented:

Training Instrument 11–16

Nominal Group Technique Case Study

In this case study we will practice implementing the Nominal Group Technique.

Instructions: Silently count the number of squares in the diagram below and write your answer on the line provided.

Answer: _____

Training Instrument 11–17
Journaling: Strategic Business Acumen

Instructions: Use the space below to complete or respond to the statements.

◆ I help apply strategic business acumen when I practice this personal strength I currently have:

◆ I would like to grow my ability to help others by applying strategic business acumen in these ways:

◆ Here are three ways I can improve my strategic business acumen:

◆ Here are ways I can leverage my strengths through strategic business acumen:

Training Instrument 11–18

Document Risk and Constraints

Instructions: For any project, only one of these constraints can be number one, two, or three at any given time. Think of a project on which you are working and prioritize Time, Cost, and Quality by entering an **X** in the block that corresponds with that priority.

CONSTRAINTS	#1	#2	#3
Time			
Cost			
Quality			

Training Instrument 11–19

Journaling: Project Leadership

Instructions: Use the space below to complete or respond to the statements.

◆ I help apply project leadership when I practice this personal strength I currently have:

◆ I would like to grow my ability to lead projects by:

◆ Here are three ways I can improve my project leadership:

◆ Here are ways I can leverage my strengths to improve my team's project leadership:

Training Instrument 11–20
Strength Worksheet

Instructions: Based on everything you have learned about your unique qualities, pick three strengths and document them using this template.

STRENGTH 1	TRIALS: STRENGTH 2	STRENGTH 3
Description:	Description:	Description:
Known successes:	Known successes:	Known successes:
Leveraging opportunities with staff:	Leveraging opportunities with staff:	Leveraging opportunities with staff:
with customers:	with customers:	with customers:
with bosses:	with bosses:	with bosses:
with vendors:	with vendors:	with vendors:
with process:	with process:	with process:
List of actions:	List of actions:	List of actions:
Top 3 goals/actions:	Top 3 goals/actions:	Top 3 goals/actions:
Measurement for top 3 actions of progress:	Measurement for top 3 actions of progress:	Measurement for top 3 actions of progress:
Intentions: 1. 2. 3.	Intentions: 1. 2. 3.	Intentions: 1. 2. 3.
Keepers of the gate:	Keepers of the gate:	Keepers of the gate:
Allies:	Allies:	Allies:
	Trials:	Trials:

Training Instrument 11–21
Opportunity Worksheet

Instructions: Based on everything you have learned about your unique qualities, pick three opportunities for improvement and document them using this template.

OPPORTUNITY 1	OPPORTUNITY 2	OPPORTUNITY 3
Description:	Description:	Description:
Known successes:	Known successes:	Known successes:
Leveraging opportunities with staff:	Leveraging opportunities with staff:	Leveraging opportunities with staff:
with customers:	with customers:	with customers:
with bosses:	with bosses:	with bosses:
with vendors:	with vendors:	with vendors:
with process:	with process:	with process:
List of actions:	List of actions:	List of actions:
Top 3 goals/actions:	Top 3 goals/actions:	Top 3 goals/actions:
Measurement for top 3 actions of progress:	Measurement for top 3 actions of progress:	Measurement for top 3 actions of progress:
Intentions: 1. 2. 3.	Intentions: 1. 2. 3.	Intentions: 1. 2. 3.
Keepers of the gate:	Keepers of the gate:	Keepers of the gate:
Allies:	Allies:	Allies:
Trials:	Trials:	Trials:

Training Instrument 11–22
Action Plan

Instructions: Translate all of the journaling and reflection you have done into an actionable plan. Set measurable goals for improvement in the first column; define how you will measure completion of the action in the second column; and note the date by which the improvement will take place in the last column.

GOAL	MEASUREMENT	DATE

Intentions:

Tool 11–1

The Hero's Journey

We are all heroes (male and female alike)—just getting up every morning and facing the day makes us heroes. And certainly navigating our way through this world of change takes incredible heroism.

Story of Origin

The place you begin: You're moving through life, minding your own business and then. . . . (Snow White is living with an evil stepmother, but seems content playing in the garden with birds, and is loved by everyone.)

Call to Adventure

Internal Calls: The little voice inside that says it's time to make a change, to take an adventure (switch jobs, move to a new place, get married or divorced). We have the choice of answering or not.

External Calls: Forces outside yourself thrust change upon you (drafted into the military, lose a loved one, hit the lottery, get fired). We have no choice in the matter (except in how we choose to handle it). (The magic mirror on the wall tells Snow White's evil stepmother that she is no longer the most beautiful; that Snow White is. This sets the stepmother into a rage and she demands that her woodsman take Snow White to the woods and kill her.)

Guardians of the Threshold

External: Those around us who try to persuade us not to answer the call to adventure; naysayers. Can be loved ones, friends, or even strangers who challenge us to defend our choices: "Why leave the company? You have such a secure job!" "You're crazy! Why do you want to do that?" "You're moving where?"

Internal: The little voice inside that says, "Don't do it!" "Why shake things up?" "Better to leave well enough alone." These voices try to persuade us out of answering our own internal calls to adventure—we have the choice not to answer the call. Some people suppress their internal calls to adventure for months, years, or even a lifetime and sometimes end up saying, "I wish I had. . . ." (The little birds try to warn Snow White about the kind woodsman's real motives, but she doesn't listen to them.)

What voices did you hear? Who were some of your naysayers?

Allies

Those who assist us in preparing for the journey: Friends, family, and strangers who contribute wisdom, strength, training, and support. Allies can appear throughout the journey. Who have your allies been? (The Woodsman, although a slave to the evil stepmother, decides to spare Snow White and pretend he has killed her.)

continued on next page

Tool 11–1, continued
The Hero's Journey

Crossing the Threshold

You ignore the naysayers and go for it: You answer the call, accept the challenge, begin your journey, and promptly find yourself in the. . . . (Suddenly, and perhaps for the first time, Snow White is alone in a deep, dark woods with nowhere to go.)

Belly of the Whale

What would it be like to be in the belly of the whale? Dark, wet, smelly, scary, lonely. It seems as though you have no control over where you are going. May seem like you'll never get out. This is like Bridges' neutral zone—a time of reflection and introspection, of finding out who you are, what you want, and what you are made of (strengths, weaknesses, dreams, visions, and identity). Being carried under water is symbolic of an internal process of discovery. (Unfortunately, Snow White does what most girls in fairy tales do: she lies on the ground and cries herself to sleep.)

Road of Trials

You've escaped the belly of the whale, but there are more challenges ahead. You are prepared to face them—you know who you are, you have vision of what you want, and you are aware of your limitations and fears. You meet the challenges and overcome them (although you may struggle with some). Each challenge offers its own learning and adds to your strength. (Snow White is startled awake by the singing of a team of seven dwarves returning from a day at the diamond mines. She decides to talk with them.)

The Accomplishment (The Gift)

Success! You have achieved what you set out to do (have slain the dragon, rescued the princess, found the buried treasure). Sometimes when you achieve success in your journey it is widely recognized and heralded (high school graduation is an example). Other times the recognition of success happens quietly—you just wake up one morning and realize that you have achieved what you had hoped (put your life back on track or adapted to the new job). (Snow White finds new happiness as the housekeeper for the dwarves. But her joy is short-lived: The magic mirror turns her in, and the evil stepmother tricks her into eating a poison apple, which causes her to fall into a deep coma. Her one true love, the prince, returns after killing the evil stepmother to find Snow White, kisses her, and she is saved.)

Magical Flight

A period of basking in the glow of your success. Cruising along, enjoying life in its new form (due to the change you've made). (Snow White and her true love ride off into the sunset together.)

Guardians of the Threshold

As you fly back to the place you began (either physically or mental/emotionally), you may encounter some of the same external naysayers. They tend to be sarcastic and try to

continued on next page

Tool 11–1, continued

The Hero's Journey

diminish your experience and growth. (Perhaps the birds warn her that she is jumping into this marriage with her true love a bit too suddenly. Perhaps the dwarves are not thrilled that she is leaving their service.)

Orchestrator of Two Worlds

You return "home" and find that everything is pretty much as you left it. You, however, are different and you cannot quite fit back into your old niche. You have one foot in each of two worlds/lives—the one you used to be a part of before the journey and the one you now belong to as a result of your growth or change. The old aspects of yourself are still there beneath the new persona you have grown into. You walk the line between these worlds until you establish a new place for yourself. (Snow White returns to the land of royalty to be a queen. Unfortunately, she has become accustomed to taking risk, living in the wilds, and pretty much having her own way. Palace life is boring and suffocating. The cycle starts again . . . .)

Once a new order has been established in your life . . . the cycle starts again.

The model is a hopeful one: You won't be in the Belly of the Whale forever. That awareness can help you track your progress through the process of transition. It can be helpful to know where you are along the way. This understanding may help you see change as an opportunity for growth.

It is important to emphasize that

- ◆ Allies change as you progress through a transition—you have different friends.
- ◆ There are critical points of crossing that roughly take you in or out of Bridge's Neutral Zone.
- ◆ Most importantly, the journey is circular and never-ending. As soon as you are "done" making the transition from one event (you probably don't even know you are done), another begins.

Luckily, we are all heroes.

Developed from Joseph Campbell's research into myths and hero stories from around the world and his book, *The Hero with a Thousand Faces.*

Tool 11–2
Systems Thinking

Slide 8–91 defines Systems Thinking and shows one loop of a Causal Loop Diagram, which can be read as follows:

As Bookings increase, Revenue also increases (the "s" indicates that the variable increases or decreases in the same way; the "o" indicates that the variable increases or decreases in the opposite way). As Revenue increases, the Investment in Sales increases (we can invest in hiring or training more salespeople). As Investment in Sales increases, Salespeople increases, which ultimately increases Bookings.

Obviously, if it were this easy everyone would be successful, so there must be other stories (loops) involved in answering such questions as "Why are our sales struggling?" The complete story is on slide 8–92. Notice that as demand increases, capacity to produce starts to run out. This triggers building new capacity, but by the time it is in place, poor delivery and poor product quality have driven down sales.

The point of Systems Thinking is that we must take a systemic view of problems. Quick fixes often make problems worse or, at best, don't improve anything. Systems Thinking allows us to look at the big picture before reacting.

Tool 11–3
Mini-Evaluation

Instructions: We want this workshop to be beneficial to you. Please take a few moments to help us adapt to your learning needs. Place a checkmark in the appropriate boxes below.

1. How do you feel about the pace of the class?

   Too fast ☐

   A little quick ☐

   Just right ☐

   A little slow ☐

   Too slow ☐

2. How do you feel about the content of the material?

   Too basic ☐

   A little basic ☐

   Just right ☐

   A little hard ☐

   Too hard ☐

3. How do you feel about the instructional style?

   Too much lecture ☐

   A little too much lecture ☐

   Just right ☐

   A few too many exercises ☐

   Too many exercises ☐

Please share any comments that you think would help the facilitator make the workshop more pertinent to you. . . . Thank you!

_____

_____

_____

_____

Tool 11–4
General Workshop Appraisal

Comments: E = EXCELLENT   VG = VERY GOOD   G = GOOD   F = FAIR   P = POOR

	E	VG	G	F	P
Instructor's presentation of the subject					
Instructor's knowledge of the subject					
Course content					
Satisfy your objectives					
Overall course appraisal					

◆ What other sessions/workshops would you be interested in attending?

◆ Are there others you feel would benefit from this workshop?

Name

Address

Phone number

Services in which he or she might be interested:

Name

Address

Phone number

Services in which he or she might be interested:

Name

Address

Phone number

Services in which he or she might be interested:

Using the Compact Disc

Insert the CD and locate the file *How to Use This CD.txt*.

Contents of the CD

The compact disc that accompanies this workbook on new employee orientation contains three types of files. All of the files can be used on a variety of computer platforms.

- **Adobe .pdf documents.** These include handouts, assessments, training instruments, and training tools.

- **Microsoft PowerPoint presentations.** These presentations add interest and depth to many of the training activities included in the workbook.

- **Microsoft PowerPoint files of overhead transparency masters.** These files makes it easy to print viewgraphs and handouts in black-and-white rather than using an office copier. They contain only text and line drawings; there are no images to print in grayscale.

Computer Requirements

To read or print the .pdf files on the CD, you must have Adobe Acrobat Reader software installed on your system. The program can be downloaded free of cost from the Adobe Website, *www.adobe.com*.

To use or adapt the contents of the PowerPoint presentation files on the CD, you must have Microsoft PowerPoint software installed on your system. If you simply want to view the PowerPoint documents, you must have an appropriate viewer installed on your system. Microsoft provides various viewers free for downloading from its Website, *www.microsoft.com.*

Printing from the CD

TEXT FILES

You can print the training materials using Adobe Acrobat Reader. Simply open the .pdf file and print as many copies as you need. The following documents can be directly printed from the CD:

- Handout 11–1: The 10 Leadership Competencies

- Handout 11–2: Chuck's Role

- Handout 11–3: Angela's Role

- Handout 11–4: Observation Checklist

- Handout 11–5: A Difficult Conversations Checklist

- Handout 11–6: Adapting Your Style: Working with Core Style D

- Handout 11–7: Adapting Your Style: Working with Core Style I

- Handout 11–8: Adapting Your Style: Working with Core Style S

- Handout 11–9: Adapting Your Style: Working with Core Style C

- Handout 11–10: The Sabotage Exercise

- Handout 11–11: Team Member Assignment Cards for the Sabotage Exercise

- Handout 11–12: Feedback

- Handout 11–13: Hints and Solutions for Feedback

- Handout 11–14: The Hero's Journey

- Handout 11–15: Delphi Technique Case Study

- Handout 11–16: Steps to Great Projects

- Handout 11–17: Define: Write the Project Definition

- Handout 11–18: Establish Project Scope

- Handout 11–19: What to Do if You're Behind

- Assessment 11–1: Leadership Self-Assessment

- Assessment 11–2: Quick n' Dirty DISC/PIAV Assessment

- Assessment 11–3: The Language System Diagnostic Instrument

- Training Instrument 11–1: Action Plan

- Training Instrument 11–2: Identification of Strengths and Weaknesses

- Training Instrument 11–3: Nine Dots

- Training Instrument 11–4: Practicing Flexibility: A Test of Your Creative Thinking Skills

- Training Instrument 11–5: Journaling: Resiliency

- Training Instrument 11–6: Journaling: Working with Others

- Training Instrument 11–7: Blending of Styles

- Training Instrument 11–8: Walk a Mile in My Shoes…

- Training Instrument 11–9: Journaling: Communication

- Training Instrument 11–10: Performance Review

- Training Instrument 11–11: Journaling: Coaching

- Training Instrument 11–12: Journaling: Vision

- Training Instrument 11–13: Change Versus Transition

- Training Instrument 11–14: Journaling: Change

- Training Instrument 11–15: Journaling: Customer Orientation

- Training Instrument 11–16: Nominal Group Technique Case Study

- Training Instrument 11–17: Journaling: Strategic Business Acumen

- Training Instrument 11–18: Document Risk and Constraints

- Training Instrument 11–19: Journaling: Project Leadership

- Training Instrument 11–20: Strength Worksheet

- Training Instrument 11–21: Opportunity Worksheet

- Training Instrument 11–22: Action Plan

- Tool 11–1: The Hero's Journey

- Tool 11–2: Systems Thinking

- Tool 11–3: Mini-Evaluation

- Tool 11–4: General Workshop Appraisal

POWERPOINT SLIDES

You can print the presentation slides directly from this CD using Microsoft PowerPoint. Simply open the .ppt files and print as many copies as you need. You can also make handouts of the presentations by printing 2, 4, or 6 "slides" per page. These slides will be in color, with design elements embedded. PowerPoint also permits you to print these in grayscale or black-and-white, although printing from the overhead masters file will yield better black-and-white representations. Many trainers who use personal computers to project their presentations bring along viewgraphs just in case there are glitches in the system.

Adapting the PowerPoint Slides

You can modify or otherwise customize the slides by opening and editing them in the appropriate application. However, you must retain the denotation of the original source of the material—it is illegal to pass it off as your own work. You may indicate that a document was adapted from this workbook, written and copyrighted by Lou Russell and published by ASTD. The files will open as "Read Only," so before you adapt them you will need to save them onto your hard drive under a different filename.

Showing the PowerPoint Presentations

On the CD, the following PowerPoint presentations are included:

- One-Hour.ppt

- Half-Day.ppt

- One-Day.ppt

- Two-Day.ppt

Table A–1

Navigating Through a PowerPoint Presentation

KEY	POWERPOINT "SHOW" ACTION
Space bar *or* Enter *or* Mouse click	Advance through custom animations embedded in the presentation
Backspace	Back up to the last projected element of the presentation
Escape	Abort the presentation
B *or* b B *or* b *(repeat)*	Blank the screen to black Resume the presentation
W *or* w W *or* w *(repeat)*	Blank the screen to white Resume the presentation

Having the presentations in .ppt format means that it automatically shows full-screen when you double-click on its filename. You also can open Microsoft PowerPoint and launch it from there.

Use the space bar, the enter key, or mouse clicks to advance through a show. Press the backspace key to back up. Use the escape key to abort a presentation. If you want to blank the screen to black while the group discusses a point, press the B key. Pressing it again restores the show. If you want to blank the screen to a white background, do the same with the W key. Table A–1 summarizes these instructions.

We strongly recommend that trainers practice making presentations before using them in training situations. You should be confident that you can cogently expand on the points featured in the presentations and discuss the methods for working through them. If you want to engage your training participants fully (rather than worrying about how to show the next slide), become familiar with this simple technology *before* you need to use it. A good practice is to insert notes into the *Speaker's Notes* feature of the PowerPoint program, print them out, and have them in front of you when you present the slides.

◆

Sample Step-by-Step
Preparation for Delivery

Here is a checklist you can use to prepare to teach any of the sessions.

SIX WEEKS BEFORE

☐ Have I spent enough time understanding the business need from my sponsor?

☐ Have I reserved the meeting space and refreshments?

☐ Have I scheduled the facilitator? (That may be you!)?

☐ Have I invited the learners?

☐ Have I instructed them on how to take the 360-degree assessment as well as DISC and PIAV assessments?

☐ Have I researched enough that I have the depth of knowledge and skill required to facilitate this material?

☐ Have I scheduled the reproduction of the materials?

ONE WEEK BEFORE

☐ Have I sent out an email reminder to all participants?

☐ Are all the supplies ready?

☐ Are all the assessments completed? Do I need to remind anyone to do it?

ONE DAY BEFORE

☐ Have I prepared my teaching notes?

☐ Have I set up the classroom?

THE DAY OF CLASS

☐ Have I arrived at least one hour early to make sure the environment is right?

ONE DAY AFTER CLASS

☐ Have I contacted all the participants to thank them for their time?

☐ Have I summarized the evaluations and sent the results to my sponsor?

Supplies List

These are the supplies that you will need for the 1–1.5-hour presentation:

ITEM	QUANTITY	USE
Copy of the presentation	One per learner	To encourage note taking and learning
Prizes	One per learner	As fun rewards for participation
Your copy of the presentation		To display as you share
Promotional materials	One per learner	To advertise the additional training available
Masking tape	One roll	To hang flipchart notes
Flipchart	One	To lead discussion
Copies of all 360-degree, DISC, and PIAV assessments	One per learner (OPTIONAL—only if using these)	In case they forget to bring them
Projection (LCD, PC, etc.)	One	For slides
Light pointer	One	For directing learners' attention to a part of a slide or overhead

These are the supplies that you will need for the half-day, one-day, and two-day workshops:

ITEM	QUANTITY	USE
Red plastic cups	One per table	To hold pencils and markers on tables
Pencils	One per learner	Place on tables for the learners' use.
Colored (scented) markers	One per learner	Place on tables for the learners' use.
Post-Its	One pad per learner	Place on tables for use during exercises.
Small pads of paper	Two per table	Place on tables for learners' note taking.
Stickers	Five sets of four different stickers (minimum two stickers per learner)	For breaking into new groups and decorating diplomas
Diplomas	One per learner	To celebrate learning
Mixed, hard candy	One bag per day of workshop	For kinesthetic learners, quick energy and for color
Sugar-free hard candy	One bag	For learners sensitive to sugar
Prizes	Two per learner per workshop day	For a fun reward
Masking tape	One roll	To hang peripherals
Learner Guide, teaching notes, and course materials		To stay focused on the objectives
Copies of all 360-degree, DISC, and PIAV assessments	One per learner	In case they forget to bring them
Roster (if possible)		For customization
Flipchart	One per table if possible	For brainstorming
Projection (LCD, PC, etc.)	One	For slides
Light pointer	One	For pointing to slides or overheads during presentations

In addition, for the two-day workshop you will need the following items:

- ◆ two decks of playing cards for every five learners (for example, 10 decks for 25 learners)

- ◆ closed clear container full of candy (counted)

- ◆ Sabotage team member assignment cards (see handouts in chapter 11)—one set for each team of four people.

Resources

BOOKS AND ARTICLES

Allen, David. *Getting Things Done: The Art of Stress-Free Productivity.* New York: Viking Press, 2001.

Barnes, B. Kim. *Exercising Influence.* Berkeley, CA: Barnes & Conti Associates, Inc., 2000.

Bridges, William. *Managing Transitions: Making the Most of Change.* Cambridge, MA: Perseus Press, 1991.

Campbell, Joseph. *The Hero with a Thousand Faces.* Princeton, NJ: Princeton University Press, 1972.

Cashman, Kevin. *Leadership from the Inside Out.* Provo, UT: Executive Excellence Publishing, 2000.

Covey, Stephen R. *The Seven Habits of Highly Effective People.* New York: Simon and Schuster, 1990.

Dahle, Cheryl. "Natural Leader." *Fast Company* 41(December), 2000.

Davenport, Thomas H., and Laurence Prusak. *Working Knowledge.* Boston: Harvard Business School Press, 1997.

Galwey, W. Timothy. *The Inner Game of Work.* New York: Random House, 1999.

Gardner, Howard. *Frames of Mind: The Theory of Multiple Intelligences.* New York: Basic Books, 1985.

—————. *Multiple Intelligences: The Theory in Practice.* New York: Basic Books, 1993.

Garfield, Charles A. *Peak Performers*. New York: HarperCollins, 1991.

Goleman, Daniel. *Emotional Intelligence: Why It Can Matter More Than IQ*. New York: Bantam Books.

—————. *Primal Leadership: Realizing the Power of Emotional Intelligence*. Boston: Harvard Business School Press, 2002.

Goss, Tracy. *The Last Word on Power*. New York: Currency/Doubleday, 1995.

Greenleaf, Robert K., with Stephen R. Covey and Larry C. Spears (editor). *Servant Leadership: A Journey into the Nature of Legitimate Power and Greatness*. Mahwah, NJ: Paulist Press, 1977.

Hammonds, Keith. "Michael Porter's Big Ideas." *Fast Company* 44(March), 2001.

Hartmann, Franz. *The Life of Philippus Theophrastus Bonbast of Hohenheim, Known by the Name of Paracelsus, and the Substance of his Teachings*. London: Wizard's Bookshelf, 1997.

Herrmann, Ned. *The Whole Brain Business Book*. New York: McGraw-Hill, 1996.

Jensen, Eric. *Brain-Based Learning*. San Diego, CA: The Brain Store, 2000.

Jones, Laurie Beth. *The Path*. New York: Hyperion Press, 1998.

Kotter, John P., editor. *What Leaders Really Do*. Watertown, MA: Harvard Business School Press, 1999.

Michalko, Michael. *ThinkerToys: A Handbook of Business Creativity*. Berkeley, CA: Ten Speed Press, 1991.

Nonaka, I. Kujiro, with Hirotaka Takeuchi, and Hiro Takeuchi. *The Knowledge-Creating Company: How Japanese Companies Create the Dynamics of Innovation*. New York: Oxford University Press; 1995.

Peters, Tom. "The Brand Called You." *Fast Company* 10(August), 1997.

Russell, Lou. *The Accelerated Learning Fieldbook*. San Francisco: Jossey-Bass, 1999.

—————. *Project Management for Trainers: Stop "Winging It" and Get Control of Your Training Project*. Alexandria, VA: American Society for Training & Development, 2000.

Russell, Lou, and Jeff Feldman. *IT Leadership Alchemy*. Upper Saddle River, NJ: Prentice Hall, 2002.

Sacks, Peter. *Generation X Goes to College: An Eye-Opening Account of Teaching in Postmodern America*. Chicago: Open Court Publishing Company, 1996.

Seligman, Martin. *Learned Optimism*. New York: Simon and Schuster, 1998.

Senge, Peter. *The Fifth Discipline*. New York: Currency/Doubleday, 1990.

——————, editor. *The Fifth Discipline Fieldbook: Stratagies and Tools for Building a Learning Organization*. New York: Currency/Doubleday, 1994.

Sittenfeld, Curtis. *"I've Seen the Future." Fast Company* 18(October), 1998.

Thiagarajan, Sivasailam (Thiagi), and Ethan S. Sanders. *Performance Intervention Maps: 36 Strategies for Solving Your Organization's Problems*. Alexandria, VA: American Society for Training & Development, 2001.

Thiagarajan, Sivasailam (Thiagi), and Glenn Parker. *Teamwork and Teamplay: Games and Activities for Building and Training Teams*. San Francisco: Jossey-Bass, 1999.

Thomsett, Rob. *People and Project Management*. Upper Saddle River, NJ: Yourdon Press/Prentice Hall, 1980.

Treacy, Michael, and Frank Wiersma. *The Discipline of Market Leaders: Choose Your Customers, Narrow Your Focus, Dominate Your Market*. Cambridge, MA: Perseus Publishing, 1997.

Vaill, Peter B. *Learning as a Way of Being: Strategies for Survival in a World of Permanent White Water*. San Francisco: Jossey-Bass, 1996.

——————. *Managing as a Performing Art: New Ideas for a World of Chaotic Change*. San Francisco: Jossey-Bass, 1989.

Wheatley, Margaret J. *Leadership and the New Science: Discovering Order in a Chaotic World*. San Francisco: Berrett-Koehler, 2001.

Yourdon, Edward. *Managing High-Intensity Internet Projects*. Upper Saddle River, NJ: Prentice Hall, 2002.

OTHER ITEMS

The MIT Organizational Learning Network. Available at http//:learning.mit.edu.

Pegasus Communications, Inc., One Moody Street, Waltham, MA 02154. Telephone: 800.272.0945; Web address: www.pegasuscom.com.

Russell, Lou. "Agile Development." Available at www.trainingsupersite.com/txx_link/trainset.html, 2001.

Russell Martin & Associates; 6326 Rucker Road, Suite E, Indianapolis, IN 46220. Telephone: 317.475.9311, Web address: www.russellmartin.com, Email: lou@russellmartin.com.

Lou Russell president and CEO of Russell Martin & Associates, a consulting and training company focusing on improving planning, process, and performance. She has served as a consultant to companies, schools, churches, and colleges to help them expand their organizational ability to learn. She is the author of *The Accelerated Learning Fieldbook, Project Management for Trainers*, and *IT Leardership Alchemy*. She can be reached via email at info@russellmartin.com.